D1411665

An Explorer's Guide to Christian Living

Journey
to the Center
of the Faith

James A. Harnish

Abingdon Press
Nashville

JOURNEY TO THE CENTER OF THE FAITH:
AN EXPLORER'S GUIDE TO CHRISTIAN LIVING

Copyright © 2001 by Abingdon Press

This book is printed on acid-free paper.

Library of Congress Cataloging-in-Publication Data

Harnish, James A.
    Journey to the center of the faith: an explorer's guide to Christian living / James A. Harnish.
        p. cm.
    Includes bibliographical references.
    ISBN 0-687-09843-2 (alk. paper)
    1. Christian life—Methodist authors.   I. Title.

BV4501.3 .H37 2001
248.4'876—dc21

2001045732

Scripture quotations, unless otherwise noted, are from the *New Revised Standard Version of the Bible,* copyright © 1989, Division of Christian Education of the National Council of the Churches of Christ in the United States of America. Used by permission. All rights reserved.

Scripture quotations noted KJV are from the King James Version of the Bible.

Scripture quotations by J. B. Phillips are from *The New Testament in Modern English, Rev. Ed.* © J. B. PHILLIPS 1958, 1960, 1972 (New York: The Macmillan Company).

Scripture quotations noted NEB are from *The New English Bible.* © The Delegates of the Oxford University Press and The Syndics of the Cambridge University Press 1961, 1970. Reprinted by permission.

Scripture quotations marked (TEV) are from the Today's English Version—Second Edition. Copyright © 1992 by American Bible Society. Used by permission.

Excerpts from *Words to Love By . . . Mother Teresa* by Mother Teresa, text compiled and edited by Frank Cunningham. Copyright © 1983 by Ave Maria Press, P.O. Box 428, Notre Dame, IN 46556, www.avemariapress.com. Used with permission of the publisher.

01 02 03 04 05 06 07 08 09 10—10 9 8 7 6 5 4 3 2 1

MANUFACTURED IN THE UNITED STATES OF AMERICA

With gratitude for the joy of
"Making God's Love Real"

with the people of
Hyde Park United Methodist Church,
Tampa, Florida

Contents

Introduction

*In the suspicious atmosphere of the contemporary Christian
church, it is good to know one's ground.*
                —Kathleen Norris, Amazing Grace, *p. 143*

I remember the day in seventh-grade science class when the
teacher—who had been around so long that our parents could
remember calling him "Pappy"—demonstrated the gyroscope. It
looked a lot like the metal top with the wooden plunger I set spinning on the linoleum-covered kitchen floor when I was a little boy.
Like most adolescent boys with a healthy libido, my seventh-grade
scientific interests were more instinctively drawn to the anatomy
of human reproduction, but this lesson in basic physics caught my
attention. I watched in amazement as he positioned the spinning
gyroscope on the very edge of his old wooden desk. He said it kept
its precarious balance because its axis did not move. Keep that stable center, he said, and it could balance on anything. Lose that center, and it would go kaput.

Decades later, I remembered that gyroscope when I discovered
some of the best-known lines from the Irish poet William Butler
Yeats. In the 1930s, while Hitler was gobbling up Europe and Great
Britain was practicing appeasement, Yeats said that "Things fall
apart; the centre cannot hold." He described a world in which
"The best lack all conviction, while the worst / Are full of passionate intensity" ("The Second Coming" in *Modern British Poetry,*
p. 117).

These words have a disturbingly familiar ring. The culture in
which we live often feels like a spinning turntable on which people are pulled to the ideological edges and farther away from any
common core of identity and belief. We may not see the "mere
anarchy" that Yeats described, but we have seen what he called
"the blood-dimmed tide" in Bosnia, in Kosovo, in the Middle East,
in parts of Africa, and on the streets and school campuses of
America. Tune in the vitriolic voices of talk radio. Take a peek at
the voyeuristic gossip of tabloid television. Follow the partisan

posturing of politicians over puny priorities. Simply take a good look at the world around us. It's difficult not to feel that Yeats somehow got it right: "Things fall apart; the centre cannot hold."

I serve as a pastor in The United Methodist Church, a "mainline" denomination that has historically been a microcosm of the culture around it. One of the unique parts of our identity has been the historic "connection" that binds us together. As we enter the new millennium, however, a variety of people representing a wide range of perspectives within the denomination are seriously questioning how much longer we can hold our connection together. Some say it is only a matter of time until the whole thing breaks apart, just the way it did in 1844 when American Methodists were divided between North and South. One of our denominational organizations has even used the word *schism* and has called upon our Council of Bishops to model a common center around which we might find some sense of unity.

Dorothy caught the spirit of our age when she woke up after the tornado and said, "Toto, I've a feeling we're not in Kansas anymore." The truth about our lives is that we are searching for a center that will hold—an inner core of conviction and belief that will enable us to keep our balance in the whirling tornado of cultural change and confusion that threatens to engulf us.

Within this spinning gyre of change, I claim to be a Christian, a person who affirms a clear center defined by faith in God revealed through Jesus Christ. In addition, I am a pastor and preacher, a very ordinary person who has been strangely set apart by the extraordinary act of ordination to lead other ordinary seekers into an extraordinary journey into the central core of Christian faith. I sometimes feel as if I am a guide in that old 20th Century Fox movie that took a team of explorers on a *Journey to the Center of the Earth*.

This book is a very personal attempt to describe a center that can hold. It bears witness to the truth about my life, the truth about the world as I see it, and the Truth as I experience it in Jesus Christ. It is a hopeful response to the soul-searing pain, the soul-searching needs, and the soul-shaping questions of people in the communities where I have lived. More than anything else, it describes a way of being Christian that I have seen take shape in the lives of real people in the congregations I have served. The models for my faith are healthy, growing, honest believers who are drawn neither to the vicious virtue of the religious right nor to the weary liberalism of the institutional left. They are on a journey to the life-giving center of the Christian faith.

Referring to the ubiquitous series of books for "dummies," a friend told me that what he needed was a book on Christianity "for dummies" to help him put into practice the things that he already believes. This book is for him and for many honest folk like him. It is a response to real questions raised by real people whose faces gather around my computer screen as I write. They are searching for a faith that makes sense in their brains and a difference in their lives. Their honesty helps to keep me centered in what I believe are the core realities of the Christian life. Their friendship along the way continues to draw me deeper into a center that will hold. I write with gratitude for each of them.

Even hard-to-impress New Yorkers were surprised to see the sign outside the Fifth Avenue Presbyterian Church that read "The Power of a Tommy Hilfiger Label." The editors of *The New Yorker* magazine wondered if the church might be attempting some sort of cross-promotion with the hottest name in designer clothing. The Reverend Thomas Tewell explained, "The models in Hilfiger ads all look so happy and vibrant. . . . We wear the label 'Christian,' and yet, for many people, our demeanor is stuffy, boring, dull, irrelevant, and holier-than-thou. So I said, hey, wouldn't it be great if we had the vitality that when people saw us they said, 'Gee, where did you get that label and how can I get it?' " (quoted in *Context*, April 15, 1997, p. 8).

I dare to hope that this attempt by one ordinary Christian to bear witness to his journey to the center of the faith will enable other ordinary Christians to live with a refreshing spiritual vitality that will cause other seekers to ask, "Gee, where can I get that?"

CHAPTER ONE

Christ-Centered:
Getting to Know Jesus

In every phase of my search, I've discovered also that Jesus
Christ stands at the center of my seeking. If you were to ask me
point-blank, "What does it mean to you to live spiritually?" I
would have to reply, "Living with Jesus at the center."
            —Henri Nouwen, Letters to Marc About Jesus, *p. 7*

It was a brilliant Palm Sunday morning on the Gulf Coast of
Florida. The rising sun sent a golden glow through the stained
glass windows and warmed the faces of the people in the congregation. Choral *hosanna*s reverberated throughout the sanctuary as
Sunday school children paraded down the aisle waving their
freshly cut palm branches. As I followed the procession to the
chancel, I looked at the faces of people with whom I had shared
times of spirit-lifting joy and gut-wrenching pain—people who
had walked the path of daring hope and heartbreaking despair;
people with whom I had shared the energizing and exhausting
process of defining the mission and vision of a local congregation
preparing for its second century of ministry. Remembering all we
had been through and realizing who, by God's grace, we were
becoming, I was drawn to the biblical text for the story the church
proclaims during Holy Week. The traditional Scripture lessons for
the day include the apostle Paul's mind-boggling challenge for
Christian people to "be of the same mind, having the same love,
being in full accord and of one mind" with this Jesus who "emp-
tied himself . . . and became obedient to the point of death—even
death on a cross" (Phil. 2:2, 7-8).

In the middle of that Palm Sunday sermon, a personal affirmation spoke itself into being in words that never appeared in the
prepared manuscript. I felt a surprising freedom from the

judgmental nature that seems to be a genetic flaw running through the generations of my family. A gracious spirit penetrated my heart as the words formed on my lips. "I know," I said, "that some folks think I'm too liberal. And I know that some folks think I'm too conservative. I want you to know that I really don't care anymore. I just want to be like Jesus. Sometimes being like Jesus means that some folks will think I'm liberal. Sometimes being like Jesus will mean that some folks will think I'm conservative. The labels just don't matter to me anymore. The only thing that matters is obedience to Jesus Christ." Looking back now, I realize how close those words were to the words of the apostle: "All I want is to know Christ and to experience the power of his resurrection, to share in his sufferings and become like him in his death" (Phil. 3:10 TEV).

My unexpected self-definition on that Palm Sunday morning was nothing short of a spiritual Declaration of Independence from the theological battle lines, political agendas, and ideological labels that tug and pull at the soul of the Christian movement in America today. It marked a fresh determination that the gravitational center of our congregation would be nothing other than the love of God revealed in the life, death, and resurrection of Jesus Christ. The identifying core of our life together would be our desire to become people in and through whose lives the Christ-centered, cross-shaped love of God would become a tangible, down-to-earth, flesh-and-blood reality. We would keep Jesus at the center and use all of our powers to live in solidarity with him.

Jesus consistently focused on people's center: Are they oriented and moving toward the center of spiritual life (love of God and people), or are they moving away from it?
—*John Ortberg,* The Life You've Always Wanted, *p. 37*

As a local church pastor, I spend a great amount of energy oiling the machinery that makes the institutional church run, but the answer to the deepest hungers of our souls will not be found in organizational systems or structures. I have invested my life in the study of Christian theology, but the gravitational center of the

Christian life is not unanimous assent to a body of intellectually comprehended beliefs. I am concerned about the moral and social values of this nation, but the Christian faith is not defined by a specific political party or agenda. I am grateful for the church that nurtured my faith, ordained me in the ministry, and appointed me to serve, but the stabilizing center for my soul is not my denominational identity.

The only clearly defined center for the Christian life is the love, life, death, and resurrection of Jesus. When I am confronted with confusing and conflicting options both inside and outside the community of faith, I find myself asking: Does it *look* like Jesus? Can I hear in this doctrine the *voice* of Jesus? Can I feel in this movement the *presence* of Jesus? Do my lifestyle, my attitudes, my relationships, my values, and my convictions reflect the compassion, joy, and wholeness of Jesus? Most important of all, am I being drawn more deeply into the central core of cross-shaped, Christlike obedience? Is my life centered in an all-consuming love for God and other people?

All I can say is, as one aging and singularly unimportant fellow man, that I have conscientiously looked far and wide, inside and outside my own head and heart, and I have found nothing other than this man and his words which offers any answer to the dilemmas of this tragic, troubled time. If his light has gone out, then, as far as I am concerned, there is no light.
—*Malcolm Muggeridge*, Jesus Rediscovered, *p. 72*

The apostle Paul said, "All I want is to know Christ." The question is, How? How can I get to know Jesus? What are the practical signposts that mark the way on a soul-journey to the center of the faith? My experience is that getting to know Jesus begins in gathering the basic information about him. The process of transformation begins by simply seeing Jesus as he is portrayed in the Gospels according to Matthew, Mark, Luke, and John.

My standard homework assignment for persons who are beginning the search for a vital faith is to encourage them to lay aside all of the images of Jesus they have collected from the remnants of Christian influence in Western culture and simply read the story in a contemporary translation of the Bible. The New Revised Standard Version is my favorite, with Today's English Version and the New International Version as runners-up. *The Message,* by Eugene Peterson, is hard to beat as a contemporary paraphrase. I encourage searchers for a vital faith to read the gospel as if they have never heard any of it before. I encourage beginners to read the Gospels the way they would read a short story. Watch what Jesus does, listen to what he says, feel the impact of his presence on the people around him, and allow his personality to emerge from the written Word. The only goal is to get to know Jesus the way the Gospel writers portray him.

But just as gathering credit card information about a customer in the checkout line is light years removed from *knowing* that same person in an intimate way, gathering information about Jesus is much different from actually *knowing* him. Knowing Jesus involves moving beyond mere information and choosing to live in spiritual solidarity with him.

Dear Jesus,
Help us to spread your fragrance everywhere we go.
Flood our souls with your spirit and life.
Penetrate and possess our whole being so utterly
that our lives may only be a radiance of yours.
Shine through us
and be so in us
that every soul we come in contact with
may feel your presence in our soul.
Let them look up and see no longer us but only Jesus.
　　　　　　　　　　—Mother Teresa, Words to Love By, *quoted in*
　　　　　　　　　　A Guide to Prayer for All God's People, *p. 49*

I am fascinated by some enigmatic characters who show up unexpectedly in John's Gospel (John 12:20-36). They were Greeks, Gentiles, people who were outside the covenant community of Hebrew faith. They were not steeped in the Hebrew Scriptures or familiar with the Hebrew traditions. They didn't know kosher from kumquats! They were just like a whole lot of folk in our culture today, ordinary people who were searching for a living relationship with God.

As the Gospel of John reports, these Greeks came to Philip, the disciple with a Greek name. He was from Bethsaida in Galilee, a city with a large non-Jewish population. My guess is that they chose Philip because they thought he might understand their search. He seemed the least likely to reject them and turn them away because of their cultural differences. Perhaps they hoped he would accept them just the way they were. They made a very simple request: "Sir, we wish to see Jesus."

I meet a lot of folk who are just like these pilgrims. They are spiritually sensitive people who know as much about being a Christian as those Greeks knew about being a Jew, and yet, they are people who are searching for a meaningful relationship with God. They couldn't care less about some of the interfamily squabbles that divide denominations or the hairsplitting issues that separate Christians. They have very little confidence in religious institutions. They just want to see Jesus!

When Philip and Andrew brought these pilgrims to Jesus, he responded to their search with a simple horticultural parable that pointed them toward the central core of the gospel: "Unless a grain of wheat falls into the earth and dies, it remains just a single grain; but if it dies, it bears much fruit" (John 12:24).

British scholar and preacher Dr. Donald English left an indelible mark on the map of my spiritual journey when he invited his listeners to imagine that we were a bunch of tulip bulbs, comfortably tucked away in a wooden box on the garden-store shelf. It's safe, dry, and warm—an altogether comfortable place to be. But one day a huge, hairy hand reaches down into the box and yanks out a handful of bulbs. The bulbs that are left behind say, "Whew! That was a close call! How fortunate that we were left behind! We have heard what will happen to those bulbs. The gardener will dig a hole in the ground and bury them in it. They will die down there, and the earth will freeze over them. We are the fortunate ones! We are still safe and secure in our cozy little box."

But Dr. English reminded us that spring would come. The snow would melt. Moisture would penetrate the earth, and those bulbs that were buried in the ground would arise to a spectacular expression of "tulipness" that the other bulbs, safety tucked away in their box, would never comprehend.

❖

Nothing that has not died will be resurrected.
—C. S. Lewis, The Weight of Glory, *quoted in*
A Guide to Prayer for Ministers and Other Servants, *p. 185*

❖

Jesus interpreted the parable with a foundational affirmation that appears, in some form, in all four Gospels: "Those who love their life lose it, and those who hate their life in this world will keep it for eternal life" (John 12:25).

"Love your life / hate your life" is, of course, a rhetorical exaggeration that points toward the central core of the Christian gospel. If we try to hold onto life—protect it, squeeze it to our chest—we lose it. But if we lose our life in the love of God in Christ, we find it. We only find life when we learn to give it away to something larger than our own self-interest.

Jesus translated the parable into his own experience: "I, when I am lifted up from the earth, will draw all people to myself" (John 12:32). Just so we wouldn't miss the point, John editorialized, "He said this to indicate the kind of death he was to die" (v. 33).

The Gospel writers are convinced that if we really want to see Jesus, we must see him on the cross, lifted up in all of his naked vulnerability and weakness. To live in solidarity with Jesus, we must go to the place where he surrendered the power and control of his life in obedience to the self-giving love of God. To know Jesus is to know him in his total identification with our human weakness and death. To meet Jesus means meeting him at the place where he entered into our human struggle and suffering. If we really want to know Jesus, we must know him at the cross—at that soul-level place where we surrender our power and control of life in obedience to the self-giving love of God. It means allowing the love of God in Jesus Christ to become the gravitational center that brings balance to all the rest of our existence.

❖

You'll meet God in the world as suffering, dying love . . . you will know that suffering, dying love is the way in which God lovingly feels his way

through the affairs of the world in order that the result might be the very
best result for everybody involved.

—The Reverend Dr. Donald English,
Proceedings of the Fifteenth World Methodist Conference
(*Waynesville, N.C.: World Methodist Council, 1986), p. 196*

It was the first week after Easter Sunday. The scent of lilies still lingered in the sanctuary, and the echo of Handel's *hallelujahs* still lingered in my soul. I was thinking of a man I knew who was going through a very intense personal struggle. He had been forced to deal with his guilt over the ways in which he had betrayed his highest ideals and broken his deepest commitments. He had been to see his counselor that morning. After listening to my friend describe his struggle with guilt and pain, the counselor had asked him, "Do you go to church?"

"Yes," my friend replied, "nearly every Sunday, almost all my life."

"Did you go on Easter?" the counselor asked.

"Yes, of course," my friend replied.

He was shocked when the counselor said, "Well, I don't know why you keep going. It certainly isn't doing you any good." Surprised by the counselor's words, my friend asked what he meant. The counselor replied, "If you really believed that Jesus died on the cross for you, you wouldn't go on acting as if you have to carry the cross yourself. If you actually believed that Jesus died and rose again to forgive you, you would find a way to forgive yourself."

My friend said it was the first time the reality of Jesus' death and resurrection made any real connection with his life. He actually felt that Jesus had entered into his struggle. Jesus had taken his failure, sin, and suffering to the cross so that he didn't have to carry it around anymore. At the cross, he felt the presence of the God in whom he had always believed. The light I saw in his face that day was something like the light of Easter morning breaking in upon an empty tomb. Like the apostle, he was beginning to know Christ in the fellowship of his suffering and in the hope of being born to new life.

Sooner or later, every journey to the center of the faith leads us to some place in our human experience that is marked by a cross—places where old parts of us must die so that something new will come to life. When we center our lives in the love of God revealed at the cross, we discover old attitudes, old prejudices, old greed, old pride, old bitterness, old habits, old selfishness, and just plain old sin—in whatever form we find it—all of which need to be nailed to the cross.

To know Christ in the power of his resurrection means that we begin to see everything—our lives, our relationships, the world around us—in a whole new way. By the power of the Resurrection, we start seeing people the way Jesus saw them, loving people the way Jesus loved them, and trusting God the way Jesus trusted the One he called Father. We come to know Jesus as we share in his sufferings, as we become like him in his death, and as we arise to new life in the Resurrection.

O Lord, give me true heavenly wisdom, that I may learn to seek you and to find you, and above all things to love you, and to understand and know all other things as they are, after the direction of your wisdom, and not otherwise.

—*Thomas à Kempis,* The Imitation of Christ,
quoted in A Guide to Prayer for Ministers and Other Servants, *p. 256*

How to Keep Jesus in the Center

1. How much do you know about Jesus? Take a fresh look at his story. Read through at least one of the four Gospels—Matthew, Mark, Luke, and John—as if you have never read it before.

2. What difference will it make for you to go beyond knowing about Jesus to living in solidarity with him? Describe the changes this would bring or require in your life. Read Philippians 2:1-8. What difference would it make for you to have "the same mind . . . that was in Christ Jesus" (v. 5)? Explain your answer as fully as possible. Read Philippians 3:7-10. What difference would it make for you to live with the same attitude that Paul expresses there? Explain.

3. What is at the center of your life? On a sheet of paper, draw a set of concentric circles—circles of different sizes around a common center—to represent the significant relationships and commitments of your life. Within the circles, write the names or brief descriptions of your relationships or commitments, placing the most important one in the center and the least important in the outer circle. What does your drawing tell you about what is at the center of your life?

4. Will you put Jesus at the center? Read Matthew 22:34-40 and John 13:31-35. What difference will it make for you to center your life in loving God and loving others as Christ loved us? Explain.

5. Have you found a place in your experience where the Jesus of history has become the Christ of experience? Has the Jesus about whom you have read become a living presence with whom you share your life? How would you need to rearrange the concentric circles of your relationships and commitments for Christ to be at their center?

Resources for Getting to Know Jesus

Bonhoeffer, Dietrich. *Christ the Center*. New York: Harper & Row, 1966.

Job, Rueben P., and Norman Shawchuck. *A Guide to Prayer for Ministers and Other Servants*. Nashville: Upper Room, 1983.

———. *A Guide to Prayer for All God's People*. Nashville: Upper Room, 1990.

Johnson, Luke Timothy. *Living Jesus: Learning the Heart of the Gospel*. San Francisco: HarperSanFrancisco, 1999.

Jones, E. Stanley. *The Divine Yes*. Nashville: Abingdon Press, 1975.

———. *Abundant Living*. Nashville: Abingdon Press, 1978.

Lewis, C. S. *Mere Christianity*. New York: Simon & Schuster, 1980.

Muggeridge, Malcolm. *Jesus Rediscovered*. Garden City, N.Y.: Doubleday, 1969.

Nouwen, Henri J. M. *Letters to Marc About Jesus*. San Francisco: Harper & Row, 1988.

Ortberg, John. *The Life You've Always Wanted*. Grand Rapids: Zondervan, 1997.

Sider, Ronald J. *Living Like Jesus: Eleven Essentials for Growing a Genuine Faith*. Grand Rapids: Baker Books, 1999.

CHAPTER TWO

Biblically Rooted:
Experiencing the Unchained Word

*J. B. Phillips, in his preface to the paraphrase he made of the
epistles, says that he felt as if he were trying to mend an electric
light system without being able to shut off the current.
Whenever we handle the Bible, we get that feeling. This is not a
dead book, it is alive, and we may get a shock at any time.*
        —D. T. Niles, The Power at Work Among Us, *p. 80.*

The evidence is overwhelming: People who find a center that
will hold are biblically rooted. They are like the people described
in the first psalm:

> They are like trees
>   planted by streams of water,
> which yield their fruit in its season,
>   and their leaves do not wither.
> In all that they do, they prosper. (Ps. 1:3)

Like a tree that is constantly growing, expanding, stretching, and
changing as it draws nourishment from the earth, people of genuine Christian faith continue to grow only so long as they continue to sink the roots of their souls deep into the words of
Scripture.

So far, so good. Many people respect the Bible, whether they
read it or not. On the other hand, the fact that "the Good Book"
continues to be "the world's best seller" is totally unrelated to the
massive biblical illiteracy that is the fundamental reality of our
time. I was reminded of that reality while preaching a series of sermons on the Old Testament story of David. The story begins with
his complex and competitive relationship with Saul, the king
David was destined to replace. After hearing me talk about Saul

for several weeks, a person who had been in worship nearly every Sunday of her life asked, "When are you going to get to the story of Saul on the Damascus road?"

If you understand the confusion in that question, you are among the rare minority of persons who know the difference between King Saul, who reigned a thousand years before the birth of Christ, and Saul of Tarsus, who became the missionary hero of the church in the first century after Christ and who was renamed Paul by Christ.

How can we respond to the biblical illiteracy of our time? How can we be biblically rooted while allowing space for the honest questions and sincere differences among faithful people? What does it mean to be biblically centered in ways that are open to dialogue and growth?

I have never known someone leading a spiritually transformed life who had not been deeply saturated in Scripture.
　　　　　—John Ortberg, The Life You've Always Wanted, *p. 177*

In his personal correspondence with Timothy, Paul used a powerful image to describe his experience of the Word of God. Paul, the apostle of Christian freedom, was a political prisoner in Rome. The missionary who had crisscrossed the Mediterranean with the liberating message of the gospel was in chains. Nearing the end of his life, he wrote, "I suffer hardship, even to the point of being chained like a criminal. But the word of God is not chained" (2 Tim. 2:9).

What powerful contrasting images! The apostle was imprisoned, but the Word of God was alive, active, freely moving—unchained! When Paul used the phrase "word of God," he was not talking about the Bible the way I received it: translated into Elizabethan English, bound in black leather with gold-leaf edges and the words of Jesus printed in red ink. Throughout the Bible, the phrase "word of God" describes God's action by which God is revealed in the created order, in covenant history, and in human experience.

The creative Word of God spoke over chaos and brought forth creation.

The covenant-shaping Word of God called Abraham and promised to make of his descendants a great people.

The liberating Word of God sent Moses to Pharaoh saying, "Let my people go."

The visionary Word of God gave the prophets a message of hope for people in bondage.

The living Word of God became human flesh in Jesus of Nazareth.

The Word of God is not chained, frozen, or static. It is the living, dynamic, life-giving self-revelation of God in action in human history that is recorded in the words of the Bible.

When the white man came to Africa we had the land and he had the Bible. And he said, "Hello." And we said, "Hello." And he said, "Let us pray." Dutifully we shut our eyes, and when we open our eyes, we discover he's got the land and we've got the Bible. But who said that was a bad bargain? We are taking the Bible seriously. . . . We tell the South African government, hey, the book that you should have banned is the Bible, but you are too late!

—Archbishop Desmond Tutu,
Proceedings of the Fifteenth World Methodist Conference, 1986, *p. 166*

For many faithful people on the religious "right," the living Word of God is chained to a rigid biblical literalism that Professor of Religion Conrad Hyers described as "a false security, a temporary bastion, maintained by dogmatism and misguided loyalty." He warned that rigid literalism "empt[ies] symbols of their amplitude of meaning and power, reducing the cosmic dance to a calibrated discussion" ("Biblical Literalism: Constricting the Cosmic Dance" in *The Christian Century*, August 4-11, 1982, p. 823).

I understand the appeal of a rigid biblical literalism. It nails things down, holds things tight, makes things secure. In a complex and confusing world, there is a simplistic security in saying, "The Bible says it! I believe it! That settles it!" But just as pinning a butterfly to a desk to study its wings kills the butterfly, biblical literalism can drain the life out of the inspired Word. It "constricts the cosmic dance" by denying the Spirit of God the freedom to move through the power and vitality of symbolic language and literature. Madeleine L'Engle called the "limited literalism" that forces all of the biblical poetry, imagery, drama, and story to be read as factual "one of Satan's cleverest devices" (*A Stone for a Pillow* [Wheaton, Ill.: Harold Shaw Publishers, 1986], p. 81).

Strict literalism that requires all truth to be historically accurate and scientifically verifiable is an assumption of nineteenth- to twentieth-century European-American rationalism that denies deeper meanings of truth that were assumed in earlier times and other cultures. The task of biblical study, under the guidance of the Spirit of God, is to listen for the ways in which the living Word of God speaks truth in the biblical text. Sometimes God speaks through verifiable historical events. Sometimes God speaks through the inspired imagery of God's action within and around those humanly verifiable experiences. Sometimes God speaks through parables, poetry, and story. Our task is to experience God's living Word through the rich variety of forms in which it comes to us through the Bible.

As a literary comparison, consider *King Lear*. Whether you can prove the historical existence of a king named Lear in no way weakens the profound truth contained in Shakespeare's greatest play. Seeing the foolish king rage against the storm or watching him attempt to push breath back into the lifeless corpse of his daughter moves us to a level of truth that is deeper and truer than any facts that could be confirmed by holding his birth certificate in our hands.

In the same sense, whether the Old Testament character of Jonah was "literally" swallowed by a particular fish on a particular day and spewed back up on a particular beach at a particular hour neither negates nor confirms the inspired truth of God's redemptive love that Jonah's story proclaims. At the same time, the historical reliability of the stories of King David or of the life of Jesus are essential to our experience of the living Word. The key to vital biblical study is allowing the text itself to determine exactly how the written word conveys inspired truth.

Rigid literalism holds its ground on the right. In the opposite corner are those for whom the Bible is merely a historical marker in an ongoing journey of religious development. By reading the Bible as a human record of subjective religious experience, people on this side of the text fail to recognize the Bible as the continuously authoritative Word for life and faith. The inevitable result is a "theology de jour" that deifies subjective experience and is taken captive by the loudest voices of the contemporary culture.

Is there a center that will hold? How can we listen for the Word of God in a way that is rooted in the continuing authority of the Scripture, while appreciating the cultural, historical, and literary forms in which it has come to us?

My journey to the center of the faith has led me to read the Bible as the inspired record of the people who experienced the active Word of God. The people of Israel received God's covenant through Abraham. The apostles experienced the Word made flesh in Jesus. The early church defined the content of the Bible as we have received it. The unchained Word of God acted. Those who experienced that action told their story in words that ultimately were written down. When we read, study, and meditate on those words, we experience the unchained, living Word in our own lives.

It [the Bible] is more than a record. It is that witness to God's saving deed which in the witnessing becomes his deed. By it and through it the incarnate, crucified, and risen Word finds his way into your life and mine. It is the history that becomes our history. It is the proclamation which brings about what it proclaims. It not only offers liberty, it sets [us] free. It does more than promise sight; it "opens blind eyes."
—Paul Scherer, The Word God Sent, *p. 33*

The Second Epistle to Timothy contains several powerful affirmations that can guide us toward a vibrant experience of the unchained Word.

Affirmation number one:

For this gospel I was appointed a herald and an apostle and a teacher, and for this reason I suffer as I do. But I am not ashamed, for I know the one in whom I have put my trust, and I am sure that

he is able to guard until that day what I have entrusted to him.
(2 Tim. 1:11-12)

Paul said, "I know whom I have believed." The primary reality in Scripture is not "how" or "what" but "who." If the Bible is the inspired witness of God's self-revelation, its purpose is to allow us to know God and to experience God's presence. The purpose of the written Word is to point beyond itself to the One whose living Word is revealed there.

When I hear what some people say about the Bible, I wonder if they've ever read it. Some folk make this fascinating collection of sixty-six books—recorded over two thousand years and written by a diverse array of God only knows how many authors—sound like Aladdin's lamp. They seem to promise that if we rub it just right and say the magic words, a divine genie will pop out with a "quick fix" for everything from politics to weight control. But that's not what the Bible promises.

The Bible promises to be the authoritative witness to God's self-revelation in history. Through that revelation, we come to know God and see God's purpose. We read the Bible with the expectation that Mary A. Lathbury expressed in her hymn "Break Thou the Bread of Life," written in 1877 for Bible study groups at the Chautauqua Institution in New York: "Beyond the sacred page I seek thee, Lord; / my spirit pants for thee, O Living Word!"

Affirmation number two:

Remember Jesus Christ, raised from the dead, a descendant of David—that is my gospel. (2 Tim. 2:8)

The central affirmation of Christian faith is that Jesus of Nazareth is God's Word made flesh, God's self-revelation in human form. The life, words, will, and way of Jesus proclaimed in the Gospels become the lens through which we read and interpret all the other words of Scripture.

Unless people are in a well-designed study process, I do not recommend that they begin at Genesis and read through the Bible. That type of reading usually falls flat by the time they reach the mildew and menstrual laws in Leviticus! I recommend that people first start their biblical journey with the Gospels—Matthew, Mark,

Luke, and John—in order to get to know Jesus. Then I encourage them to move forward to hear the formative witness of the early Christian church in the book of Acts and the Epistles. Readers of the Bible are then prepared to move backward to experience the long history of God's self-revelation in the Old Testament. Finally, they are ready to look ahead to the final fulfillment of God's purpose in the Technicolor images in Revelation.

The Bible then is not the revelation of God. It is the inspired record of the revelation. Otherwise, the revelation—the word become flesh—would be printer's ink. The revelation is seen in the face of Jesus Christ.
—E. Stanley Jones, The Divine Yes, p. 39

Affirmation number three:

Remind them of this, and warn them before God that they are to avoid wrangling over words, which does no good but only ruins those who are listening. (2 Tim. 2:14)

The apostle knew our human tendency to get tied up in the small print and miss the big picture of God's saving action in human history. It seems we tend to come to the Bible the way the "nearsighted" cat in the nursery rhyme went to London:

> Pussycat, pussycat,
> where have you been?
> I've been to London
> to visit the queen.
> Pussycat, pussycat,
> what saw you there?
> I saw a little mouse
> run under the chair.

We need to keep our eyes on the queen-sized story of God's saving action in human history and allow the mouse-sized details to take care of themselves. The big story is God's faithfulness to God's saving purpose in a world that is broken and bruised by the rebellion we call sin. The big story is the way God chooses to save and redeem the world through divine grace and self-giving love.

Affirmation number four:

> Continue in what you have learned and firmly believed, knowing from whom you learned it, and how from childhood you have known the sacred writings that are able to instruct you for salvation through faith in Christ Jesus. (2 Tim. 3:14-15)

Ideally, being biblically rooted means that from the earliest days of our children's lives, they are nurtured on the words of Scripture, hearing the stories of Moses and Noah, Ruth and Esther, David and Jesus. As they grow up with the written Word, they begin to experience the living Word. As they continue to live with and listen to the words of Scripture, it will progressively become the living Word at the center of their lives. Paul continues: "All scripture is inspired by God and is useful for teaching, for reproof, for correction, and for training in righteousness, so that everyone who belongs to God may be proficient, equipped for every good work" (2 Tim. 3:16).

To say that the Bible is inspired does not mean that God dictated the text to passive notetakers who wrote down whatever God told them to write. Inspiration is closer to the Genesis writer's poetic description of the way God took a lifeless lump of clay and breathed into it the breath of life (Gen. 2:7). *Inspired* means that God's presence became the controlling reality in the clay of human experience. Out of that living experience with God, the biblical witnesses told their story and finally recorded this written Word. The Spirit is alive within it, in part because it comes right out of the common clay of our human experience with God. The Old Testament emerged out of the tumultuous history of the people of Israel; it is filled with doubt and faith, despair and hope, failure and success, forgiveness and guilt. The New Testament originated in the shared life of the early Christian community, which struggled to bear witness to the death and resurrection of Jesus Christ in a hostile and pagan culture.

Both Testaments are filled with real, genuine, honest human emotions. When our guts are twisted in pain, when we are angry or afraid, when we bubble over with exuberant joy, when we experience guilt and failure, when we long for justice and peace, when we search for a vision of the future, it's all in there. We can find ourselves and God's action in our lives within the pages of this book.

Kierkegaard used to say that most of us read the Bible the way a mouse tries to remove the cheese from the trap without getting caught. . . . The way you do that is to read it as if it were a story about somebody else a long time ago. . . . But if you interpret it, if you get the sense of it, if you seek for the meaning of it, then you will read it as a story of God searching for you. Look for someone in the text who is like you. Then look out.

—Mark Trotter, "The News That Stays New,"
sermon preached January 23, 1983

God breathed the breath of life into the common clay of our human experience. In the same way, God breathes life into the recorded experience of these people. When we study, listen, and live with this book, it becomes the living, dynamic, life-changing Word of God in our experience, too.

I remember a young man who started coming to our church when he was a sophomore in high school. He was obviously brilliant, with an exceptionally high IQ, always questioning, always searching for knowledge. He had not grown up in the church and had only minimal exposure to Christian faith. In an advanced program at a university in Great Britain, he took a course in comparative religions and decided to read the Bible. After that reading, he wrote me a thirteen-page letter recording his initial impressions. I was amazed by the way he captured the earthy humanity and the divine vitality of the Scriptures.

About two weeks ago I read the Bible from Genesis to Revelation. . . . I really must say that it was quite an eye opener. . . . When I first picked up the Bible I expected it to be a lot more sober than it actually was. . . . I really loved how lusty everyone was. . . . Apparently the chosen people had a great libido. . . . I was expecting some drab story about Satan and heaven. What I got was a wonderfully vivid story about real people in a hostile world.

When he experienced the story of the return of the exiles in Nehemiah, he remarked, "What guts! I really loved every minute of it." Although he did not particularly like the book of Proverbs, his response captured some of the basic characteristics of wisdom literature:

> The majority [of the proverbs] were just plain strange and about twenty of them caused me to burst into uncontrolled laughter. . . . I did notice two things. One, they all tried to keep the status quo. . . . Second, if I ever get into a bad situation I can quote any one of these proverbs and then walk off and no one will know what I said but they would all think that I had said something.

At the end of his reading of the Old Testament, he wrote, "I was really able to laugh and cry through it and plan on rereading it in the near future. . . . I really did get quite an education. . . . I don't think there is anything quite like it." He shared the same kind of honest, open reactions to the New Testament and then wrote: "I was surprised to find out how interesting it was. . . . I cannot get over how diverse it all was. . . . I have a foundation."

An agnostic philosopher named Emile Cailliet described a similar experience of the living presence of God in his first encounter with Scripture.

> I read, and read, and read. . . . I could not find words to express my awe and wonder. And suddenly the realization dawned upon me: This *was* the Book that would understand me. . . . I continued to read deeply into the night, mostly from the Gospels. And lo and behold, as I looked through them, the One of whom they spoke, the One who spoke and acted in them, became alive to me. (*Journey into Light*, p. 18)

Both the student and the philosopher—like Timothy before them—experienced within the written Word the unchained Word of God as the living, vibrant reality of God's revelation, each in his own experience. And so can we!

Enlighten me, Lord Jesus, with the clarity of everlasting light, and drive out of my heart all manner of darkness and all vain imaginations and violent temptation. . . .

Send out your light and your truth of spiritual knowledge, that it may shine upon the earth, barren and dry. . . . Give me the water of inward devotion to moisten the dryness of my soul, that it may bring forth good fruit. . . . Make me one with you in a sure bond of heavenly love, for you alone are sufficient to your lover, and without you all things are vain and of no substance.

—*Thomas à Kempis,* The Imitation of Christ, *quoted in* A Guide to Prayer for Ministers and Other Servants, *pp. 256-57*

How to Experience the Unchained Word

1. Describe your honest feelings about the Bible. What place does it hold for your faith? How much actual experience have you had with it? What types of experiences have you had with the Bible? Describe them.

2. What comes to mind when you hear the phrase "Word of God"? How does the definition of the phrase "Word of God" given in this chapter fit in with your previous understanding of that phrase?

3. What does it mean to say that the Bible is truth? Do you require all truth to be historically accurate and scientifically verifiable? How does your understanding of truth limit or expand the power of the "unchained Word" in your life?

4. Think about each of the four affirmations from 2 Timothy offered in this chapter. How have you experienced them in your study of the Bible? How do they create a framework for your future growth?

5. Peter Gomes writes of "the risk and the joy of the Bible: risk in that we might get it wrong, and joy in the discovery of the living Word becoming flesh" (*The Good Book*, p. xiii). How have you experienced the risk and the joy of the Bible?

6. The Bible is a "community" book that emerged out of the experience of a people of faith. It is best understood and applied when it is shared with a community of faithful people who join us in the search for truth. The most effective way to hear the Word of God in Scripture is to become a member of a small-group Bible study in which you can share your search with other people of faith. Disciple Bible Study is an excellent resource for such a group. In what ways do you understand or have you experienced the Bible in community with others?

Resources for Experiencing the Unchained Word

Brueggemann, Walter. *Finally Comes the Poet*. Minneapolis: Fortress Press, 1989.

Cailliet, Emile. *Journey into Light*. Grand Rapids: Zondervan, 1968.

Capon, Robert Farrar. *Hunting the Divine Fox*. New York: Seabury, 1974.

Gomes, Peter J. *The Good Book: Reading the Bible with Mind and Heart*. New York: William Morrow, 1996.

Jones, E. Stanley. *The Divine Yes*. Nashville: Abingdon Press, 1975.

Niles, D. T. *The Power at Work Among Us*. Philadelphia: Westminster Press, 1967.

Scherer, Paul. *The Word God Sent*. New York: Harper & Row, 1965.

Willimon, William H. *The Intrusive Word*. Grand Rapids: Eerdmans, 1994.

CHAPTER THREE

Kingdom-Visioned:
Living the Future Today

*We believe that [the kingdom of God] can only come into exis-
tence through the power of the spirit of Jesus working in our
hearts and in the world. The one important thing is that we be
as thoroughly dominated by the idea of the Kingdom of God as
Jesus required His followers to be.*
—Albert Schweitzer, Out of My Life and Thought, *p. 56*

The day I could not make out my friend's face on the stage of
the Tampa Bay Performing Arts Center was the day I knew the
time for new glasses had come. I had held out long enough under
the illusion that I wasn't actually that old. But now I had no choice.
I made my appointment and within a few weeks had been fitted
with a new pair of bifocals. And I must confess that they have
helped. Now I can see if the folk in the back row of the sanctuary
fall asleep during the sermon! The medical diagnosis was myopia;
I'm nearsighted. I can see things clearly if they are within arm's
reach, but I have difficulty seeing things farther away. And that is
precisely the spiritual ailment Jesus diagnosed in those who gathered around him: "Seeing they do not perceive, and hearing they
do not listen, nor do they understand" (Matt. 13:13).

Jesus quoted from the call of the Old Testament prophet Isaiah
(see Isa. 6:9-10):

> You will indeed listen, but never understand,
>   and you will indeed look, but never perceive.
> For this people's heart has grown dull,
>   and their ears are hard of hearing,
>   and they have shut their eyes. (Matt. 13:14-15)

Jesus diagnosed our common human ailment as "spiritual

myopia." We share a common, human tendency to become so narrowly focused on the immediate that we cannot see the eternal, so centered in the present that we cannot envision the future, and so limited by what has been that we become blind to what could be. By contrast, Jesus told his disciples, "To you it has been given to know the secrets of the kingdom of heaven. . . . Blessed are your eyes, for they see, and your ears, for they hear" (Matt. 13:11, 16).

People who are on a journey to the center of the Christian faith discover that their vision is improving. As they center their lives in the will and way of Jesus Christ, they find that their spiritual myopia is being healed. They are ordinary people with extraordinary spiritual vision to see the kingdom of God coming here and now on earth, even as it is already fulfilled in heaven.

[The kingdom] is already an accomplished fact in Jesus himself. We are invited not to make it happen, but to believe that it is and to let it come.
—Robert Farrar Capon, The Parables of the Kingdom, *p. 46*

Jesus talked about the kingdom of God more than he talked about any other single subject. The best way to comprehend what he was talking about is to begin at the end. Kingdom-centered people have eyes to see all of life from the perspective of the ultimate fulfillment of the purpose of God in human history.

In an earlier book on the Minor Prophets of the Old Testament, I confessed that I am a compulsive "last-page reader." It's almost impossible for me to read a novel or biography without taking a peek at the last page to see where the whole thing will end. I went on to say that "the prophets of Israel read the book of human experience from the perspective of the final page on which they could see the ultimate triumph of God" (*God Isn't Finished with Us Yet,* Upper Room, 1991, p. 100).

In that same prophetic spirit, Jesus taught his disciples to see the present in terms of the future—to see life as it is from the perspective of the way God intends for it to be. He gave them eyes to see the kingdom—the gracious rule, the loving authority, the redemptive purpose—of God becoming a reality in the very real, very finite world in which they lived. He called them to seek first that kingdom at the very core of their being and to become a contrast community through which the rule and reign of God could be modeled in this world.

The vision of God's future contained in the words of the Hebrew prophets, the parables of Jesus, and the dreams (and nightmares!) of John in the Revelation lifts our eyes beyond the present to the ultimate fulfillment of God's purpose in human history. The biblical vision is clear. We know what will be on the last page.

> Then I saw a new heaven and a new earth; for the first heaven and the first earth had passed away, and the sea was no more. And I saw the holy city, the new Jerusalem, coming down out of heaven from God, prepared as a bride adorned for her husband. And I heard a loud voice from the throne saying,
> "See, the home of God is among mortals.
> He will dwell with them;
> they will be his peoples,
> and God himself will be with them;
> he will wipe every tear from their eyes.
> Death will be no more;
> mourning and crying and pain will be no more,
> for the first things have passed away." (Rev. 21:1-4)

George Frideric Handel placed the promise of God's reign at the center of his "Hallelujah!" chorus (see also Rev. 11:15 KJV):

> The kingdom of this world
> Is become the kingdom of our Lord,
> And of His Christ, and of His Christ;
> And He shall reign for ever and ever.

When Christian people gather in worship, they affirm the promise in the Nicene Creed: "He will come again in glory to judge the living and the dead, / and his kingdom will have no end." Biblical faith knows what is on the last page. Our challenge is learning how to live faithfully in the pages that will continue to turn until then. What does it mean for us to live in the present in ways that are consistent with what we envision for the future?

For the Christian, therefore, holiness is the fruit of our association with Jesus. It seems to set us apart, not in the sense of being other-worldly, but rather in the sense of being grasped by the Kingdom vision that formed the center of Jesus' life and message.

—*James C. Fenhagen,* Invitation to Holiness,
quoted in A Guide to Prayer for All God's People, *p. 266*

One of the biblical deficiencies of the eschatological, endtime, or Second Coming chatter floating around as we have entered the new millennium is that it separates the apocalyptic visions of the Revelation from the real-life commands of Jesus in the Gospels. The most concise picture of Jesus' vision of life in the reign of God is recorded in two different settings in the New Testament. Matthew's version is the most familiar: "When Jesus saw the crowds, he went up the mountain; and after he sat down, his disciples came to him. Then he began to speak, and taught them" (Matt. 5:1-2).

We call Jesus' following discourse the Sermon on the Mount because that's where Matthew—good Hebrew that he was—placed it: on the mountain, similar to the way Moses went to the mountain to receive the Ten Commandments. In Matthew's account, Jesus sits down to teach, like a rabbi in the synagogue. Writing to people who saw themselves as the chosen and elect, Matthew has Jesus share his teaching in the intimacy of his hand-picked disciples.

Luke, who wrote as a Gentile to a Greek audience, offered a different setting. Jesus did not stay on the mountain, but "came down with them and stood on a level place" (Luke 6:17). In contrast to Matthew's smaller group of chosen people, Luke's crowd is a motley crew that includes everyone and anyone who wanted to hear. The slightly more spiritual tone in Matthew gives way in Luke's narrative to a very visceral, human setting. "They had come to hear him and to be healed of their diseases; and those who were troubled with unclean spirits were cured. And all in the crowd were trying to touch him, for power came out from him and healed all of them" (Luke 6:18-19).

Though there are significant differences in their accounts, both

Matthew and Luke share the same purpose. They are drawing together Jesus' essential teachings on the kingdom of God in ways that enable us to see the rule of God being actualized in down-to-earth, human experience. It is impossible to read either account without sensing that Jesus actually expects his followers to live this way!

> Then he looked up at his disciples and said:
> "Blessed are you who are poor,
>   for yours is the kingdom of God.
> "Blessed are you who are hungry now,
>   for you will be filled.
> "Blessed are you who weep now,
>   for you will laugh.
> "Blessed are you when people hate you, and when they exclude you, revile you, and defame you on account of the Son of Man. Rejoice in that day and leap for joy, for surely your reward is great in heaven; for that is what their ancestors did to the prophets." (Luke 6:20-23)

It may well be that the salvation of our world lies in the hands of the maladjusted.
                        —*Martin Luther King Jr.,* A Testament of Hope, *p. 216*

We might as well admit it: the kind of kingdom living Jesus described in the Sermon on the Mount just doesn't fit in our world. It's a lot like a suit I saw in the men's store window. From the sidewalk, it looked perfect. But when I actually tried it on I discovered that the arms were too long and the shoulders were too big. It was more suit than I could wear.

If we are really honest, aren't we sometimes tempted to look at the Sermon on the Mount the way I looked at that suit in the men's store window? From a distance it looks just right. We recognize it as something we need and may even believe that it describes the way life will be ordered at the end of time. We sometimes tend to elevate the Beatitudes (Jesus' blessings found in Matt. 5:3-12) to an ethereal mountain of spirituality, safely removed from the gritty realities of the world in which we live. But when Jesus stands with us on the "level plane" of human experience, when we hear him speak these words in the crowded confusion of our diseased, troubled, and tormented world, we may be all too quick to decide that this kingdom vision "just doesn't fit." Just try this suit on for size:

"Love your enemies, do good to those who hate you, bless those who curse you, pray for those who abuse you. If anyone strikes you on the cheek, offer the other also" (Luke 6:27-29).

Stanley Hauerwas, preacher, author, and professor at Duke University, said, "To put it as contentiously as I can, you cannot rightly read the Sermon on the Mount unless you are a pacifist" (*Interpretation*, April 1993, p. 153). In this incredibly violent world, how many of us really want to wear that suit? Or try this on for size:

"Give to everyone who begs from you; and if anyone takes away your goods, do not ask for them again. Do to others as you would have them do to you." (Luke 6:30)

"If you love those who love you, what credit is that to you? For even sinners love those who love them. If you do good to those who do good to you, what credit is that to you? For even sinners do the same. If you lend to those from whom you hope to receive, what credit is that to you? Even sinners lend to sinners, to receive as much again. But love your enemies, do good, and lend, expecting nothing in return. Your reward will be great, and you will be children of the Most High; for he is kind to the ungrateful and the wicked. Be merciful, just as your Father is merciful." (Luke 6:32-36)

Is there a single member of a church committee on finance who would seriously suggest that we practice that kind of economics? Or what about this vision of human sexuality:

"You have heard that it was said, 'You shall not commit adultery.' But I say to you that everyone who looks at a woman with lust has already committed adultery with her in his heart. If your right eye causes you to sin, tear it out and throw it away; it is better for you to lose one of your members than for your whole body to be thrown into hell. And if your right hand causes you to sin, cut it off and throw it away; it is better for you to lose one of your members than for your whole body to go into hell." (Matt. 5:27-30)

Without returning to the worst abuses of Victorian restraint, what will it mean for us to live by a kingdom-vision of the sacredness of human sexuality in our sexually saturated, sensually manipulated, love-starved culture?

Jesus opens our eyes to a vision of life that contradicts the most closely held traditional cultural values of our society. It is a vision of life that just doesn't fit the world in which we live. And yet, these words paint the picture of the way Jesus expects his disciples to live if they are to know and experience the reign and rule of God in human experience. His words define the way God intends for human life to be experienced today, even as they lift before us the vision of the way things will be when God's purpose is accomplished at the end of time.

Now and then we catch a glimpse of the rule of God coming on earth as it is already fulfilled in heaven, but all too often we have a difficult time knowing what to do with it. Once upon a time, not so very long ago, we elected a born-again, Sunday school-teaching, Bible-believing president who actually thought that Jesus meant for us to take the Sermon on the Mount seriously. It sounded good at first, but in less time than it takes to grow a good crop of peanuts, the American people (many of them born-again, Sunday school-teaching, Bible-believing Christians) decided that what looked good at a distance simply did not fit the political realities of the White House. I suspect that someday church historians will look back and say that one of the great ironies of our time was the way many folk on the "religious right" rejected Jimmy Carter and chose to align themselves with a narrow political agenda. But they won't be alone. To this day, many people in our nation have a hard time knowing what to do with Jimmy Carter.

Jim Wooten, senior correspondent for ABC News, acknowledged as much in *The New York Times Magazine*. Reflecting on the former president's peacemaking efforts in North Korea, Haiti, and Bosnia, he described Carter as a man who is "drawn to intractable problems, to lost causes and impossible dreams," and who is "no stranger to failure"; "he does what he does . . . as an exercise in high morality, altogether genuine and sincere." Wooten acknowledged that in America today Carter is "mocked as sanctimonious or silly, phony or foolish, naïve or meddlesome."

People can't seem to understand when Carter insists that it's very simple for him: "I have one life and one chance to make it count for something. I'm free to choose what that something is, and the something I've chosen is my faith. . . . My faith demands—this is not optional—my faith *demands* that I do whatever I can, wherever I can, whenever I can, for as long as I can with whatever I have to try to make a difference" (*The New York Times Magazine*, January 29, 1995, pp. 28, 30).

Jimmy Carter grew up hearing the Sermon on the Mount in Sunday school and believes that Jesus expects his followers to live that way. Secular historians can assess his role as a political leader, but as a follower of Jesus, he has modeled life in the kingdom of God in a practical and powerful way.

The Kingdom of God is a head-on and total answer to [humanity's] total need, individual and collective. It is the most radical proposal ever made to this world of ours: it proposes to replace this present unworkable world order, founded on greed and strife, with God's order—the Kingdom of God. . . . When you obey the laws of the Kingdom written within you . . . you obey that for which you are made; this Kingdom is your homeland.
—E. Stanley Jones, A Song of Ascents, *p. 386*

But *how*? How do we find healing for our spiritual myopia? How do we begin to orient our lives around the biblical vision of the kingdom of God? What are the first steps toward a life that is centered in the hope of God's reign?

Hanging on the wall of my study, just above my computer, is a framed document that declares that on August 20, 1891, Fritz Hornbach, a native of Germany, "exhibited a petition praying to be admitted a citizen of the United States." He declared that "he did absolutely and entirely renounce and abjure all allegiance and fidelity to any Foreign Prince, Potentate, State or Sovereignty whatsoever" and that he would "support the Constitution of the United States." Because of that oath, he became a citizen of the United States.

Fritz was my great-grandfather. When he took the oath of citizenship, there could be absolutely no doubt in his mind that swearing allegiance to the United States meant a clear rejection of loyalty to any other power. Saying "yes" to his new life in America meant saying "no" to the rule under which he had lived in Germany.

In the same way, claiming our identity as citizens of the kingdom of God requires the surrender of all other loyalties to the redemptive rule and loving authority of God. Saying "yes" to God's reign includes a decisive "no" to everything that is less than God's best purpose for our lives and for the created order. Centering our life in Christ means bringing every relationship, every loyalty, and every commitment under the controlling power of God's reign that became flesh among us in Jesus of Nazareth. It calls for a radical reorientation of the fundamental values by which we live in the present and a total redirection of the overruling vision by which we are called to the future. It calls us to lifelong learning as disciples of the master teacher.

The healing alternative to the spiritual myopia of our time is a renewed vision of the kingdom of God and a life-shaping desire to see it come on earth, in us, today, even as it is already fulfilled in heaven. "To you," Jesus said, "it has been given to know the secrets of the kingdom of heaven. . . . Blessed are your eyes, for they see, and your ears, for they hear."

How to Become a Kingdom-Visioned Person

1. What is your definition of the kingdom of God? How has this chapter confirmed or changed that definition?

2. What do you believe the last page of human history will hold? What does the promise of Revelation 11:15 mean for your life? What does it mean for you to affirm the words of the creed: "[Christ] will come again in glory to judge the living and the dead"?

3. How does what you believe about the future shape the way you live in the present? Be as specific as possible in your answers.

4. Read Matthew 5–7 and Luke 6:17-49. Do you think Jesus really meant for us to live this way? Explain your answer.

5. From your own experience, name a person who models the reign of God, and describe the ways in which this person does so.

6. What kind of changes would you need to make in your life to model the kingdom of God coming on earth as it is already fulfilled in heaven?

Resources for Seeing the Kingdom

Capon, Robert Farrar. *The Parables of the Kingdom*. Grand Rapids: Zondervan, 1985.

Harnish, James A. *God Isn't Finished with Us Yet*. Nashville: Upper Room, 1991.

Jones, E. Stanley. *The Unshakable Kingdom and the Unchanging Person*. Nashville: Abingdon Press, 1972.

———. *The Christ of the Mount*. Nashville: Abingdon Press, 1981.

———. *A Song of Ascents: A Spiritual Biography*. Nashville: Abingdon Press, 1968.

King, Martin Luther, Jr. *A Testament of Hope: The Essential Writings and Speeches of Martin Luther King, Jr.,* edited by James M. Washington. San Francisco: HarperSanFrancisco, 1986.

Snyder, Howard A. *Models of the Kingdom.* Nashville: Abingdon Press, 1991.

Willard, Dallas. *The Divine Conspiracy.* San Francisco: HarperSanFrancisco, 1998.

CHAPTER FOUR

Spirit-Animated:
Letting the Spirit In

There was a far greater reality in all this, the sense of the presence of a Person; not exteriorized in space, not standing opposite one, or inside one, or outside one, not standing here or there or anywhere, but living in the midst. . . . You know that Christ is born within you . . . That you can love! That you are standing on the threshold of infinite possibilities!
   —*Thomas Merton,* A Thomas Merton Reader, *p. 157*

To tell the truth, I don't lose much sleep worrying about atheism these days. I haven't run into an honest-to-goodness, red-blooded, flesh-and-blood atheist in years.

These days the most basic theological issue for people on a journey to the center of the faith is not atheism but spirituality. Futurist theologian Leonard I. Sweet quoted Harold Bloom in saying that ours is a "religion-soaked" society (*Faithquakes*, p. 117). Sweet compared our culture to a starved body that cannot be expected to have discriminating culinary tastes. It will consume almost anything. "Starved and stunted souls, restless and unearthed," Sweet says, "are searching for the touch that will turn them on, the taste that will fill them up, the spark that will catch them on fire" (*Quantum Spirituality*, p. 92).

I was among a group of church leaders gathered for supper at the Rainforest Cafe in a Chicago suburb. After a full day in a high-energy conference on evangelism and church leadership, we were ready for a night out. Perhaps we'd even take in a movie. A woman at the table engaged the twenty-something waiter in an animated conversation about the latest movies. In the process, she noticed the tattoo that wrapped itself around his arm. When asked about it, the young man pulled up his sleeve and described the artwork, which, he said, would cost over $700 by the time it was completed. We did not get to see the way the figures spread up over his shoulder to the middle of his back. He explained the tattoo by say-ing, "These are my three gods" as he pointed out the form of the god of wisdom, the god of strength, and the god of love. He said that the tattoo assured him that his gods were always with him. The woman who had initiated the conversation said, "We believe in one God." His response was characteristic of his generation. He said, "Oh sure, I believe in that god, too."

The critical challenge of our time is to define the character of our spiritual experience, to clarify the central core of our spiritual iden-tity, to name the spirit within. We are challenged to answer these questions: What kind of God is at the center of your faith? Who lives in you?

The modern era bred doubt. Its burning question was God's existence. . . . The postmodern era breeds superstition. Its burning question is God's presence. Our problem today is not doubt and disbelief, but false belief. People believe anything and everything.
　　　　　　　　　　　　—*Leonard I. Sweet,* Faithquakes, *p. 117*

Imagine yourself, your personality, who you really are, as a house. Any kind of house will do, just as long as it is custom-designed for you. It may be a huge castle with lofty turrets and waving banners. It may be a rustic mountain cabin beside a gur-gling stream. My soul-home looks like a Florida "cracker" house (named for an architectural style typical of early settlers of our state), situated beside a wide, lazy river, with cane-backed rocking chairs on a huge front porch and the sound of the summer breeze rustling through lush palm branches. When you have that house clearly pictured in your imagination, imagine a visitor walking up to the entrance and pushing the button for the doorbell, clanking the knocker, or rapping on the door. When the door opens, who will the visitor find inside?

Who lives in *you*? Some people give me the distinct impression that no one is at home. They seem empty, hollow, devoid of any spiritual presence to animate their faces or energize their souls. They remind me of how Jesus looked at the crowds who gathered around him and said they were like sheep without a shepherd.

Other people I have observed remind me of the man who, when Jesus asked his name, replied, "My name is Legion; for we are many" (Mark 5:9). And though that man's personal circumstances were different from mine, his words certainly explain how it is for me. My parents are at home in me. I inherited my mother's emotional energy and her love for music. I can see my dad's integrity, his addictive work ethic, and his quiet determination at work in my life. As my wife and I have watched our daughters become women, it has been amazing (and at times frightening!) to see that so much of ourselves is alive in them. Other people who have influenced my life are at home in my personality, too. Professors who stretched my mind, friends who made me laugh, soul-companions who nurtured my faith. I understand what Alfred, Lord Tennyson meant when he wrote, "I am a part of all that I have met" ("Ulysses" in *Writers of the Western World*, p. 783).

Who lives in you? Your answer may be a door through which to enter the apostle Paul's life-transforming prayer for the Ephesian Christians:

> I bow my knees before the Father, from whom every family in heaven and on earth takes its name. I pray that, according to the riches of his glory, he may grant that you may be strengthened in your inner being with power through his Spirit, and that Christ may dwell in your hearts through faith, as you are being rooted and grounded in love. I pray that you may have the power to comprehend, with all the saints, what is the breadth and length and height and depth, and to know the love of Christ that surpasses knowledge, so that you may be filled with all the fullness of God. (Eph. 3:14-19)

The vague, self-oriented, "squishy" spirituality of our contemporary culture demands that we think clearly about the essential character of the God who lives in us. The center of Christian faith toward which we are moving is more than a religious creed or a collection of doctrines to which we give mental assent. The life to which Jesus calls his followers is deeper than moral principles or cultural values by which we shape our actions. Being a part of the Body of Christ goes beyond joining a community of like-minded people. Life in the kingdom is not defined by a vague sort of spirituality that floats around about halfway between reality and fantasy. The transforming power at the center of the Christian faith is a living relationship with the one-and-only, for-all-time, original God whose essential character has been revealed to us in Jesus Christ. Through that relationship, the same love, the same compassion, the same Spirit of God that was alive in Jesus of Nazareth takes up residence in us. Let's take a closer look at what this means.

❖

"Christ in me" means Christ bearing me along from within, Christ the motive-power that carries me on, Christ giving my whole life a wonderful poise and lift, and turning every burden into wings. . . . To be "in Christ," to have Christ within, to realize your creed not as something you have to bear but as something by which you are borne, this is Christianity.

—*James Stewart,* A Man in Christ,
quoted in A Guide to Prayer for All God's People, *p. 154*

❖

First, Paul prays that we "may be strengthened in [our] inner being with power through his Spirit" (Eph. 3:16). J. B. Phillips's paraphrase speaks of "the strength of the Spirit's inner re-inforcement."

I watched in amazement as—after years of preparation by the congregation—the contractor poured the foundation of the sanctuary for St. Luke's United Methodist Church. The architect called it a monolithic slab. The full weight of the building rests on four pillars that carry all of the structural stress of the building into the concrete slab, where hundreds of feet of reinforcing steel bars hold the whole thing together. You can't see it now, but it's all under there. Those steel bars are the inner reinforcement that will enable the building to withstand the winds of a Florida hurricane. In the same way, Paul prays that we will know the inner strength of the Spirit of God that can hold life together in the storms.

Second, Paul prays "that Christ may dwell in [our] hearts through faith, as [we] are being rooted and grounded in love" (3:17). He prays that we will comprehend with all other Christians "the breadth and length and height and depth" of the love of God, a love that goes completely beyond human comprehension. In the

Christian tradition, the purpose of spiritual discipline is to allow the same love that we see in the words, the way, the life, and the cross of Jesus to become the controlling influence at the center of our personality. The goal is to allow the living Christ to take up residence in us.

At Walden, Henry David Thoreau offered his call to "simplify, simplify." As I get older, some things are becoming simpler. Not easier, but simpler. Here's one. If asked how to pick out the Christians in a crowd, I would not start with doctrine or theology. I would not begin with how well they know their Bible. I would not check out their positions on social issues. I would not even ask if they are active in the church. I would get around to those things, but that's not where I would begin. I would begin with Christlike, cross-shaped love. Christians are ordinary people in whom God's extraordinary love is becoming a living, breathing, growing, working reality by the power of God's Spirit. Isn't that exactly what Jesus said as he shared his last Passover supper with the disciples? "I give you a new commandment, that you love one another. Just as I have loved you, you also should love one another. By this everyone will know that you are my disciples, if you have love for one another" (John 13:34-35).

Just allow people to see Jesus in you.
                              —*Mother Teresa*, Words to Love By,
            quoted in A Guide to Prayer for All God's People, *p. 271*

The love by which Jesus said his disciples would be known is the love that met a despised tax collector named Zacchaeus and said, "Come down; I must stay at your house today" (Luke 19:5). It is the love that met a woman caught in the act of adultery and said, "Neither do I condemn you. Go your way, and from now on do not sin again" (John 8:11). It is the love that heard the cry of a dying criminal on a cross and said, "Today you will be with me in paradise." It is the love that prays for all of us, "Father, forgive them; for they do not know what they are doing" (Luke 23:34). The only unimpeachable sign of the Spirit of Christ within us is the cross-shaped, self-giving love of God shaping our values, determining our goals, directing our decisions, and animating our whole being.

Third, Paul prays that we will be "filled with all the fullness of God" (Eph. 3:19). Someone asked me recently what it means to be "filled with the Holy Spirit." I said it means that every inch of my personality, every fiber of my being, is soaked, saturated, drenched, and permeated with the love of God that we see in Jesus Christ. The questioner continued, "If we have been filled with the Holy Spirit, can we lose it?" All I could say was that I know what it means to be filled with the Spirit, and I also know that I leak! I know times when Christ's love flows through my personality in compassionate, energizing, and joyful ways. But I also know times when my soul runs dry, when compassion is the last emotion I experience, when joy is a distant memory.

When Paul talked about being filled with the Spirit, he was not describing a momentary, ecstatic experience. He was not prescribing a spiritual vaccination that we "get" and "have" for the rest of our lives. He was not fantasizing about some form of esoteric spirituality that is totally out of touch with reality. He was calling us to a dynamic relationship with God in which the love of Christ becomes so real, so alive, so much a part of our personalities that it influences every decision, shapes every action, touches every relationship we share. The love of God becomes the energizing center out of which the rest of our life flows.

But how does it happen? What practical steps can we take to nurture the life of the Spirit within us?

There is nothing original, complex, or surprising about the practical steps to spiritual growth. They are as easily accessible as they are easily ignored. Richard J. Foster outlined the experience-proven patterns of "The Path to Spiritual Growth" in his book *Celebration of Discipline*, which has become a basic primer for spiritual formation in our time. He described "The Inward Disciplines" (meditation, prayer, fasting, and study), "The Outward Disciplines" (simplicity, solitude, submission, and service), and "The Corporate Disciplines" (confession, worship, guidance, and celebration). In my own journey, I have found three essential disciplines to be the bare minimum for my soul-survival.

Discipline number one: concentrated reflection on the Scriptures. I have found no substitute for thoughtful, disciplined, personal meditation on the written Word. The "squishy spirituality" of our culture has demonstrated that we may be very "religious" without the Bible, but we will never find our way to the center of a vital and transforming relationship with God in Christ without a growing, disciplined, intentional study of the written Word. A living experience of God's presence in our lives is nurtured as we soak ourselves in the words and spirit of the biblical text. My own pattern involves both the use of the Common Lectionary, which provides assigned scriptural texts for each week of the liturgical year, and guided meditation in resources such as *The Upper Room Disciplines.*

Discipline number two: personal solitude and prayer. I can miss my personal quiet time for a day or two and still feel the presence of the Spirit of God living in me. But if I fail to keep my time alone with God, I inevitably find myself running on my own resources, depending on my own judgment, and generally ending up making a mess of things. I end up feeling dry, empty, and drained of spiritual power. I need my quiet time each morning about as much as I need my first cup of coffee. My soul needs my times of prayer the same way my body needs its regular run down Bayshore Boulevard beside the Hillsborough Bay. For more than a decade I have used *A Guide to Prayer for Ministers and Other Servants* and *A Guide to Prayer for All God's People,* edited by Bishop Rueben Job, as the essential pattern for my time alone with God. The best resource I have found for persons who are just beginning to develop their life of prayer is *The Workbook of Living Prayer* by Maxie Dunnam.

Discipline number three: intimate Christian friendship. My personality-test scores prove what my friends already know: I am an extrovert. That means I draw strength from being in relationship with other people. In times of struggle, conflict, joy, or pain, my experience of God's presence in my life has been shaped and strengthened by my relationships with trusted brothers and sisters in Christ. Their friendships and faith have been the source of most of my spiritual growth. Their part in the maintenance of my spiritual health is a direct parallel to the part my two running partners play in the maintenance of my physical conditioning. Sometimes my accountability to them is the only thing that gets me out of bed in the morning. Running with them pushes me to go farther than I would choose to go on my own. And there is always someone there to celebrate when I'm better today than I was yesterday.

So, who lives in *you*? I still remember a certain teenager, though decades have passed since I met him. I was the guest speaker for his church's "Youth Week," and he had attended every session. In the closing worship time, we invited the kids to share what they had learned or experienced. His hand was the first to go up. "I've learned," he said, "that Christ can really live in me." And like him, you can learn that this is true for you in your life as well!

O come and dwell in me, Spirit of power within,
and bring the glorious liberty from sorrow, fear, and sin.

Hasten the joyful day which shall my sins consume,
when old things shall be done away, and all things new become.
—Charles Wesley, "O Come and Dwell in Me" in
The United Methodist Hymnal, *no. 388*

How to Experience the Spirit Within

1. What signs do you see of the spiritual hunger of our times? How do you experience that hunger in your own life?

2. In your imagination, picture the "house" of your soul. Who lives in you? Name the persons who have most deeply shaped, influenced, or marked your life.

3. How have you experienced the love, compassion, or joy of the Spirit in your own life?

4. Reflect on the three essential disciplines outlined in this chapter. How have you practiced these disciplines in your life? What steps could you take to begin to practice them?

5. Describe a person who is your soulmate or the type of person you would like to have for a soulmate. Reflect on how you might search for spiritual soulmates who will join you in a small group for spiritual growth. (Two excellent resources for this are Richard J. Foster's *Celebration of Discipline* and Maxie Dunnam's *The Workbook of Living Prayer*.)

6. Spend some quiet time of reflection on the hymn by Charles Wesley at the end of this chapter.

Resources for Living in the Spirit

Dunnam, Maxie. *The Workbook of Living Prayer*. Nashville: Upper Room, 1977.

Foster, Richard J. *Celebration of Discipline: The Path to Spiritual Growth*. San Francisco: HarperSanFrancisco, 1988.

Harper, Steven. *Devotional Life in the Wesleyan Tradition*. Nashville: Upper Room, 1995.

Job, Rueben P., and Norman Shawchuck. *A Guide to Prayer for All God's People*. Nashville: Upper Room, 1990.

Merton, Thomas. *A Thomas Merton Reader*, edited by Thomas P. McDonnell. New York: Image Books/Doubleday, 1974.

Mogabgab, John, ed. *Communion, Community, Commonweal: Readings for Spiritual Leadership*. Nashville: Upper Room, 1995.

Peterson, Eugene. *Subversive Spirituality*. Grand Rapids: Eerdmans, 1997.

Sweet, Leonard I. *Quantum Spirituality: A Postmodern Apologetic*. Dayton, Ohio: Whaleprints, 1991.

———. *Faithquakes*. Nashville: Abingdon Press, 1994.

CHAPTER FIVE

Open-Minded:
Opening the Doors of Our Minds

> *Touched by the lodestone of thy love,*
> *Let all our hearts agree,*
> *And ever toward each other move,*
> *And ever move toward thee.*
> —Charles Wesley, *"Jesus, United by Thy Grace"*
> *in* The United Methodist Hymnal, *no. 561*

Listen closely and you will hear a disturbing sound blasting across the airwaves of talk radio, shouting from a bumper sticker in midtown traffic, screaming from the lips of hard-rock singers, burning in the homiletical hostility of angry preachers, and lurking under the subtle bigotry of single-issue politicians. A woman in an Ohio congregation heard it. She told her pastor that the loudest and most painful noise in our nation today is the sound of minds snapping shut all over America. She went on to make the point by saying, "Too many of us are becoming people whose minds are closed and whose opinions are set in a sort of fatal concrete which threatens to sink the fragile nature of our democracy" (Ronald M. Paterson, quoted in *Homiletics*, July-September, 1994, p. 14).

There is consensus about very little in America today—except perhaps that there is no consensus, and that we live in an increasingly polarized and vitriolic culture. No matter what the issue, the first voices to be heard are the most extreme and divisive, speaking the politics of contempt that has become so pervasive.

> —Kyle A. Pasewark and Garrett E. Paul,
> The Christian Century, *August 24-31, 1994, p. 780*

Tragically, some of the most polarized and vitriolic voices in our culture are those of people who sincerely believe that they are the sole proprietors of Christian virtue. Committed Christian people side up against one another, often divided over issues that Jesus never mentioned and for which the biblical support is exceptionally thin. I have observed that when people begin drawing circles to define who is "in" and who is "out," they always begin with the assumption that they themselves are "in."

We can take some consolation in knowing that Jesus' first disciples struggled with the same temptation. They were on their way to Jerusalem, where Jesus had already announced that he would face the cross, when Jesus overheard them arguing about which disciple was the greatest. Jesus asked, "What were you arguing about on the way?" (Mark 9:33). There must have been a long, uncomfortable silence—the kind of silence we all experience when we get caught with our hand in the cookie jar of our own self-centeredness. Simply realizing that Jesus saw their self-orientation was enough to convict them. Jesus did not rub their noses in their selfish pride or beat them over the head with their sin. Instead of speaking directly to them, he modeled a different way of living under the reign and rule of God. He took a child in his arms and said, "Whoever welcomes one such child in my name welcomes me" (Mark 9:37).

What does it mean to welcome a child? We immediately think of all the wonderful things about children: their innocence, laughter, freedom, and sheer amazement at everything. But as every parent knows, welcoming a child also means welcoming messy diapers, sleepless nights, and a whole lot of fingerprints on the glass-topped coffee table. No family welcomes a new child without changing the way they live. My wife and I call it "child-proofing" the house. Welcoming a child means taking that child just the way he or she is and adapting your life to the changes that child brings.

My favorite moment in the movie *Forrest Gump* occurs early in the picture. Forrest is telling the story of the first time he climbed on the school bus. Making his way down the aisle, he is rejected at every seat. Then he remembers, "I heard the most beautiful sound I had ever heard." A little girl said to him, "You can sit here." If the most painful noise in our nation today is the sound of minds snapping shut, then one of the most beautiful sounds must be the word

Jesus uses in Mark 9:37: "welcome." It means, "Come on in; you can be yourself here."

One of the most beautiful sounds I hear is when people say they feel a Christlike welcome in the congregation I serve. They describe a sense of genuine acceptance for who they are; they don't have to put on some kind of phony spirituality or religious façade. They do not feel required to line up with a specific political agenda. They feel that they can come in, sit down, and be at home. They describe finding a place in the community of faith where they can share the honest struggles of their souls, the genuine searching of their faith, and the reality of their human feelings and emotions. It is a living expression of the way Jesus welcomes us.

Deep passions and the importance of what's at stake conspire to raise the level of discourse to a babel of arrogant certainties, as though terribly complex issues could be hammered into simplicity by increasing the volume of argument. . . . Our culture—including the church within it—could use a massive infusion of what Richard Mouw calls "uncommon decency."
—Donald W. McCullough, The Trivialization of God, pp. 59-60

Unfortunately, the disciples didn't get the point. When Jesus said welcoming children in his name meant welcoming him, John replied, "Teacher, we saw someone casting out demons in your name, and we tried to stop him, because he was not following us" (Mark 9:38). Jesus did not respond with a lecture on the insidious influence of prejudice and spiritual bigotry. He simply pointed to an alternative way of behavior. "Do not stop him; for no one who does a deed of power in my name will be able soon afterward to speak evil of me. *Whoever is not against us is for us*" (Mark 9:39-40, emphasis added).

The prevailing mood of our culture encourages us to turn Jesus' words in the opposite direction. We're tempted to say, "Whoever is not *for* us must be *against* us." Christian fundamentalism in America emerged as a reaction to the "modernist" movements at the turn of the century and the inroads of scientific and technological knowledge. Within its genes is a tendency to fear anyone who does not share the same assumptions, live by the same convictions, or affirm the same doctrines. The result is an underlying assumption that those who see things differently are at best mistaken and are in fact probably wrong.

Growing up on those assumptions, I inherited a clear sense that whoever was not for us had to be against us. I found myself going into the world fearfully, defensively, expecting it to be full of enemies. As I have moved toward the center of life in Christ, I have found myself also moving closer to the affirmative spirit of Jesus' words: "Whoever is not against us is *for* us." When I have gone into the world with that positive expectation, I have found it to be full of friends.

Does this mean that "anything goes" in the kingdom of God? Does it mean that there are no boundaries to truth and no limits to moral and ethical behavior? Am I suggesting that we throw away our traditions, toss overboard our doctrines, and deny the real differences between us? Of course not! Jesus' words do not encourage us to be weak in our convictions, but they do call us to be Christlike in our relationships. He challenges us to allow the love of God to break through the barriers we erect between ourselves and others, so that we can welcome other people with the same kind of loving acceptance with which Christ welcomes us.

"Have salt in yourselves," Jesus said (Mark 9:50). Go ahead—be salty! In other words, be perfectly clear about what you believe and the convictions by which you live. But Jesus also said—sensing that once we get the salt shaker in our hands, we may overdo it—"be at peace with one another." If the ugliest sound in the land is the sound of doors slamming in the faces of people who aren't like us, then one of the most beautiful sounds must be the sound of doors opening to others in a spirit of peace.

I beseech you, in the bowels of Christ, think it possible you may be mistaken.
> —*Oliver Cromwell, quoted in* Context, *July 15, 1991, p. 4*

I'd like to think that the disciples got the message that day and that they all lived happily ever after, but that's not the way it worked. The history of the early church in the New Testament book of Acts tells the story of faithful people who continued to wrestle with the racial, cultural, and religious differences that separated them. Just take a look at the events recorded in Acts 10:1-33, 11:1-18, and 15:1-35. Listen to Paul's concern in 1 Corinthians 1:10-31. Feel the passion in Peter's directive to "always be ready to make your defense to anyone who demands from you an accounting for the hope that is in you" (1 Pet. 3:15).

"Making my defense" came naturally for me. I grew up in a family of world-class debaters. One of my World War II–veteran uncles served in the Army, one in the Air Force, and one in the Navy. I remember long arguments about which branch of the service actually won the war. I inherited their genes and was raised to be a vigorous debater, well groomed in defending my position. As a child of the 1960s, my political convictions were forged on the anvil of rigorous debate, nationwide protest, and profound political tension. When it comes to "making my defense," I have always needed to hear the rest of Peter's words: "yet do it with gentleness and reverence" (1 Pet. 3:16). That attitude of gentleness and respect for others is the definitive style of men and women who are centered in the love of God revealed in Christ.

The way of response calls for commitment to the God revealed in Jesus Christ—and openness to the surprising ways this God has acted beyond exclusive circles.
—Martin E. Marty, By Way of Response, *pp. 141-42*

"Finally," Peter said, "all of you, have unity of spirit, sympathy, love for one another, a tender heart, and a humble mind. Do not repay evil for evil or abuse for abuse; but, on the contrary, repay with a blessing" (1 Pet. 3:8-9).

A person who seemed to question my theological purity once asked, "Which is more important to you: truth or tolerance?" The question took me by surprise. I had never thought about that sort of separation. As best I remember, I replied that if I believe that the truth of God is revealed in Jesus, a gracious spirit of loving tolerance of others is a central element of the truth I most deeply believe. My deepest desire is to become a tenderhearted person who relates to those who hold differing convictions with humility and love that are centered in the Spirit of Christ.

John Wesley was a spiritual leader with strong convictions. He never hesitated to defend the hope that was within him. One of the reasons he published his sermons was to clearly define the content of his faith and belief. But it was no accident that he included in his first collection of sermons two companion sermons on the subject of Christlike, open-minded love for other Christians. "A Caution Against Bigotry" was based on the same story from Mark's Gospel that we have studied in this chapter. In this sermon, Wesley wrote:

> Are you on God's side? Then you will not only not forbid any man that casts out devils, but you will labour, to the uttermost of your power, to forward him in the work. You will readily acknowledge the work of God, and confess the greatness of it. You will remove all difficulties and objections, as far as may be, out of his way. . . . And you will omit no actual proof of tender love, which God gives you an opportunity of showing him. (*Works of John Wesley,* vol. V, p. 490)

Looking into his own soul, Wesley declared: "Search me, O Lord. . . . Look well if there be any way of 'bigotry' in me. . . . O stand clear of this! . . . Think not the bigotry of another is any excuse for your own" (*Works of John Wesley,* vol. V, p. 491).

The second sermon, "Catholic Spirit," has become something of a classic in the Methodist tradition. In it Wesley, describing a person who is filled with the love of Christ, wrote:

> He is fixed in his congregation as well as his principles. He is united to one, not only in spirit, but by all the outward ties of Christian fellowship. . . . His heart is enlarged toward all mankind, those he knows and those he does not; he embraces with strong and cordial affection, neighbours and strangers, friends and enemies. This is catholic or universal love. . . . Love alone gives the title to this character. (*Works of John Wesley,* vol. V, p. 503)

Elsewhere in this same sermon, Wesley wrote: "Though we cannot think alike, may we not love alike? May we not be of one heart, though we are not of one opinion? Without all doubt, we may" (*Works of John Wesley,* vol. V, p. 493).

It would be difficult to improve upon the model of Wesley's

"catholic spirit" as a redemptive alternative for our world today. If the ugliest sound in the land is the sound of minds snapping shut, then one of the most beautiful sounds must be the sound of the doors of our hearts, our minds, and our relationships opening to other persons in the Spirit of the living, loving Christ.

The question . . . is "How do I sing my song to Jesus with abandon, without telling dirty stories about others?"
  —*Leonard I. Sweet quoting Krister Stendahl in* Faithquakes, *p. 182*

How to Develop an Open Mind

1. How have you heard or experienced the sound of minds snapping shut across our country?

2. How can you identify with the disciples in Mark 9:33-34? When have you shared their feelings? Search your own soul for how deeply you need to know that you are the greatest. At what conclusions do you arrive?

3. When and where have you experienced the kind of welcome that Forrest Gump received on the school bus (described in this chapter)? When and where have you extended this kind of welcome to someone else?

4. Read 1 Peter 3:8-16. What is the practical impact of this passage on the way you relate to people who disagree with you?

5. After reflecting on John Wesley's words, how would you express his intention in your own life?

Resources for Having an Open Mind

Marty, Martin E. *By Way of Response*. Nashville: Abingdon Press, 1981.

McCullough, Donald W. *The Trivialization of God: The Dangerous Illusion of a Manageable Deity*. Colorado Springs: Navpress, 1995.

Peck, Scott. *A World Waiting to Be Born*. New York: Bantam, 1993.

Wallis, Jim. *The Soul of Politics*. New York, N.Y. and Maryknoll, N.Y.: The New Press and Orbis Books, 1994.

———. *Who Speaks for God?* New York: Delacorte, 1996.

Wesley, John. "A Caution against Bigotry," "Catholic Spirit." *The Works of John Wesley*, Volume V. Grand Rapids: Zondervan, 1959.

CHAPTER SIX

Warmhearted:
Receiving a New Heart

*The heart itself is but a small vessel, yet dragons are there, and there are
also lions; there are poisonous beasts and all the treasures of evil. But there
too is God, the angels, the life and the kingdom, the light and the apostles,
the heavenly cities and the treasuries of grace—all things are there.*
—*Pseudo-Macarius, quoted in Kathleen Norris's* The Cloister Walk, *p. 125*

The history of every century begins in the heart of a man or woman.
—Willa Cather, O Pioneers! *quoted in the* New York
Public Library Book of 20th Century American Quotations, *p. 233*

A few years ago *Time* magazine reported the story of a
Michigan farmer who received a new heart. After a twenty-year
battle with heart disease and four years of waiting, he was
bumped to the top of the heart transplant list when his daughter
was killed in a car accident in Tennessee. Doctors removed her
heart, packed it in ice, and flew it six hundred miles to Michigan
where, six hours later, it began beating in her father's chest. It
made headlines because it was the first time that a heart was trans-
planted from one family member to another.

According to Ezekiel, God is in the heart transplant business.
The Old Testament prophet heard God say, "A new heart I will
give you, and a new spirit I will put within you; and I will remove
from your body the heart of stone and give you a heart of flesh"
(Ezek. 36:26).

The heart is the biblical symbol for the motivating core, the life-
giving nucleus, the governing and controlling center of our being.
The heart is "mission control" for human life and experience. Any
journey to the center of the faith ultimately leads us to the heart.
The work of God within us is to replace our hard hearts with
warm, compassionate, loving hearts—hearts that are sensitive to
the Spirit, gentle in their convictions, and loving in their relationships with others.

❖

*By heart . . . I mean the center of our being, that place where we are most
ourselves . . . where we are most real.*
                         —*Henri Nouwen*, Letters to Marc About Jesus, *p. 5*

❖

The heart was where John Wesley placed the central emphasis in
early Methodism. The Reformed theological tradition began with
the brain, centering faith in correct belief. What mattered most was
defining the faith and getting it right. But John Wesley, drawing on
his Anglican roots and influenced by the Moravians, focused on
the heart. He wrote:

> Neither does religion consist [of] . . . right opinions; which,
> although they are not properly outward things, are not in the heart,
> but the understanding. A man may be orthodox in every point . . .
> he may assent to all the three Creeds . . . and yet it is possible he
> may have no religion at all. . . . This [the religion of the heart] alone
> is religion, truly so called. . . . Thou shalt hear and fulfil His word
> who saith, "My son, give me thy heart." And, having given him thy
> heart, thy inmost soul, to reign there without a rival, thou mayest
> well cry out, in the fulness of thy heart, "I will love thee, O Lord, my
> strength." . . . True religion [is] a heart right toward God and man.
> (*Works of John Wesley*, vol. V [Grand Rapids: Zondervan, 1959], pp.
> 78-80)

In the Wesleyan tradition, the heart of the matter is always a
matter of the heart. Faith begins with the heart and moves toward
the brain. At the risk of oversimplification, the purpose of the spiritual life is to get the heart right in relationship with God and then
to spend the rest of our lives working out the way our brain under-
stands it. It is the lifelong process by which God gives us a new
heart.

One of the most accurate terms we use to describe this work of
God's Spirit in our hearts is *conversion*. My working definition of
that term came from an accountant who said he would not be in
worship one Sunday morning because his corporation was going
through a conversion. I said, "Wait a minute—that's *my* word!
What do you mean by *conversion?*" He explained that they were
installing a new computer system and that the process of changing

from the old system to the new was called "conversion." After the conversion, everything would be different because they would operate under an entirely new program.

It's too bad Ezekiel didn't know about computers! That's exactly the process he was describing. He heard God say, "I will remove from you the heart of stone." The hard-hearted internal program that determined our past behavior on the basis of our own self-orientation will be removed. "And I will give you a heart of flesh." God promises the gift of a new program that will enable you to operate in a new way, with a heart of flesh, like the heart of the Word that became flesh in Jesus Christ. It's like receiving a new heart.

In the Reagan era, Lee Atwater was known and feared as the brutal, hard-hearted, win-at-all-costs chairperson of the Republican National Committee. Then he was diagnosed with brain cancer. Suddenly, his perspective changed. Near the end of his life he said, "I acquired more [wealth, power, and prestige] than most. . . . But you can acquire all you want, and still feel empty. It took a deadly illness to put me eye to eye with that truth, but it is a truth that the country, caught up in its ruthless ambitions and moral decay, can learn on my dime. . . . What is missing in society is what was missing in me: a little heart" (*Soul Cafe*, February 1995, p. 5).

In conversion a new life is introduced into the conscious mind as we consciously accept Christ as Savior and Lord. A new love and a new loyalty flood the conscious mind. The subconscious mind is stunned and subdued by this new dominant loyalty to Christ.
　　　　　　　　　　　　　　　　—E. Stanley Jones, Song of Ascents, *p. 52*

How does conversion happen? How can we receive a new heart? How can we get rid of the heart of stone and receive a heart of flesh? Mr. Wesley offered three very practical steps.

Step number one: Wesley challenged us to "first . . . know thyself to be a sinner. . . . [Know that] Thy will is . . . distorted . . . averse from all good, from all which God loves, and prone to all evil" ("The Way to the Kingdom"). Further, Wesley urged us to "acknowledge, with our heart as well as lips, the true state wherein we are" ("The Righteousness of Faith").

Wesley began the conversion process at the same soul-place King David described in Psalm 51. In the background of this passage is the tragic story of deceit, lust, murder, and political intrigue revolving around David's sordid affair with Bathsheba. You can read the R-rated account in 2 Samuel 11–12. When David faces up to his sin, here is how he prays:

> Have mercy on me, O God,
>   according to your steadfast love;
> . . . .
> Wash me thoroughly from my iniquity,
>   and cleanse me from my sin.
> For I know my transgressions,
>   and my sin is ever before me. (Ps. 51:1-3)

Our stories may not be as colorful or dramatic as David's story, but a journey to the center of the faith always involves a deep awareness of the radical self-orientation within us that we call sin. When we look into our heart of hearts, into the core of our being, we know our estrangement from God, from ourselves, and from others. We know the huge gap between what our best selves believe we ought to do and what we end up doing. We know the insidious power of radical self-centeredness. When we tell the truth, we know how C. S. Lewis felt when he looked inside himself and discovered "a zoo of lusts, a bedlam of ambitions, a nursery of fears, a harem of fondled hatreds" (*Surprised by Joy*, p. 226).

Theologians call it "original sin." That phrase does not mean "original" in the sense of new or unique. When someone asks if I believe in original sin, I usually tell them that I keep looking for an original sin but end up repeating the same *old* ones! We mean "original" in that it is original equipment on every model that comes off the line. We all have it.

National Public Radio storyteller Garrison Keillor once described his beloved townsfolk in Lake Wobegon by saying that left to their own devices, they would inevitably head straight for the small potatoes. Likewise, left to our own devices, we invariably head toward things that are less than God's best will for our lives. One of the most effective spiritual leaders I know confessed that if he were left on his own, his leadership would become demonic. He sensed a downward pull toward greed, a magnetic attraction to selfishness, an inner tug toward arrogance and pride. Wesley referred to it as "the inbred corruption of the heart." Ezekiel called it a "heart of stone." Whatever image we use, the first step toward a new heart is to acknowledge that we are hard-hearted sinners who are in need of a new heart.

Step number two: Wesley calls us to "repent," to "submit to the righteousness of God," to "give him thy heart." Listen to the way David described that process.

> You desire truth in the inward being;
>   therefore teach me wisdom in my secret heart.
> Purge me with hyssop, and I shall be clean;
>   wash me, and I shall be whiter than snow.
> . . . .
> Create in me a clean heart, O God,
>   and put a new and right spirit within me. (Ps. 51:6-7, 10)

It was not enough for that Michigan farmer to acknowledge that he needed a new heart. It was not enough for his daughter's heart to be carefully transported from Tennessee to Michigan. He had to submit to the operation. To receive the new heart, he had to let go of the control of his own life and trust himself to the surgeons' hands. If we want to know the divine transplant of God's Spirit within us, it will require a profound surrender of the innermost part of our being to the transforming power of the love of God revealed in Jesus Christ. Martin Luther, the sixteenth-century reformer, called it "the Joyful Exchange." It is the joy-bringing exchange of an egocentric, hard-hearted self for a God-centered, warmhearted one.

Christian conversion involves a radical transformation of the inner core of our lives, a profound reordering of our priorities, a powerful redirection of our deepest loves and loyalties, a complete surrender of all that we know of ourselves to all that we know of God's love in Christ. Henri Nouwen describes it as "a complete interior turnaround" in which every step we take draws us closer to the inexhaustible love of God (*Letters to Marc About Jesus*, p. 61). It's like receiving a new heart.

For C. S. Lewis, "the Joyful Exchange" happened quietly and unexpectedly while he was riding up Headington Hill on the top of a bus. God offered him what he later remembered as "a moment of wholly free choice":

> Without words and (I think) almost without images, a fact about myself was somehow presented to me. I became aware that I was holding something at bay, or shutting something out. Or, if you like, that I was wearing some stiff clothing, like corsets, or even a suit of armor, as if I were a lobster. I felt myself being, there and then, given a free choice. I could open the door or keep it shut; I could unbuckle the armour or keep it on. Neither choice was presented as a duty; no threat or promise was attached to either, though I knew that to open the door or to take off the corslet meant the incalculable. The choice appeared to be momentous but it was also strangely unemotional. . . . I chose to open, to unbuckle, to loosen the rein. . . . I felt as if I were a man of snow at long last beginning to melt. (*Surprised by Joy*, pp. 224-25)

The process of conversion always involves a moment of free choice in which we surrender ourselves to the invasive power of the love of God in Christ.

Step number three: Wesley calls us to "aim at the best end by the best means" ("The Righteousness of Faith"). He wrote: "The one perfect Good shall be your one ultimate end. . . . One design you are to pursue to the end of time,—the enjoyment of God in time and in eternity. Desire other things, so far as they tend to this" ("The Circumcision of the Heart").

The purpose of a heart transplant is not to prepare a person to die, but to prepare a person to live. The purpose of the divine heart transplant is not just to prepare us to go to heaven but to enable us to live on earth the way we will one day live in heaven. The Spirit of God gives us new love, new joy, new compassion, new energy, and a whole new sense of the Spirit of the living, loving, laughing Christ alive in the motivating core of our being. New living is the reason for a new heart.

There should be an impatience in the Christian life. We should not be content for the Kingdom and the life of perfect love to be postponed.
—*Gordon Wakefield in* The English Religious Tradition and the Genius of Anglicanism, *p. 190*

I grew up among Christian folk who spent a lot of energy debating whether God's saving work in human experience is a crisis or a process. Does conversion happen all at once, or is it something that happens over a long period of time? The Wesleyan answer is: "Yes."

Yes, conversion involves crisis. There are critical moments when we know ourselves and make a fresh surrender of our hearts to the love of God. There are defining moments when we turn in a new direction. There are times when we come to that place where, to quote Robert Frost, "two roads diverge in a yellow wood," and our choice of which road to take makes all the difference.

And yes, conversion is process. The new life of God within us is going somewhere. God always has new love for us to experience, new compassion for us to share, new paths for us to follow, new surrenders for us to make, and new realizations of God's kingdom taking shape among us. God always has more to do in our lives. Conversion means aiming for the best end by the best means. John Wesley called this process "sanctification," or being made perfect, complete, or whole in love. Charles Wesley set that affirmation to music when he wrote:

> Finish, then, thy new creation; pure and spotless let us be.
> Let us see thy great salvation perfectly restored in thee;
> changed from glory into glory, till in heaven we take our place,
> till we cast our crowns before thee, lost in wonder, love, and praise.
> ("Love Divine, All Loves Excelling" in *The United Methodist Hymnal*, no. 384)

A person who experienced the inner gift of a new heart in the life of our congregation shared this witness with me:

> Dear Jim,
>   My story of how I started attending Hyde Park United Methodist is somewhat a sad one, but [it] is really no longer that important. I want you to know that my focus as a person has changed since I started coming to church. I want to live my life the way Jesus would want me to. I have much to learn, but I have the rest of my life to learn it. More and more before I make a crucial decision, I ask myself, "Is this the way Jesus would handle this?" I'm not always sure of the answer, but I will become more sure as I learn more about our faith.

A new heart. That's exactly what God wants for each of us!

O grant that nothing in my soul
May dwell but thy pure love alone;
O may thy love possess me whole,
My joy, my treasure, and my crown;
Strange flames far from my heart remove;
My every act, word, thought, be love.
　　　—Paulus Gerhardt, quoted in The English Tradition
　　　　　　and the Genius of Anglicanism, *p. 174*

How to Receive a New Heart

1. What does the heart symbolize for you?

2. Does your faith experience begin in the brain and go to the heart? Or does it begin in your heart and go to your brain? What difference does it make for you to see your faith in this perspective?

3. What does the word *conversion* mean for you? How have you experienced it?

4. Walk through John Wesley's steps for receiving a new heart as outlined in this chapter. How have you experienced these steps?

Resources for New Hearts

Harper, Steven. *Embrace the Spirit*. Wheaton, Ill.: Victor Books, 1987.

Jones, E. Stanley. *Victory Through Surrender*. Nashville: Abingdon Press, 1971.

———. *Conversion*. Nashville: Abingdon Press, 1978.

———. *Growing Spiritually*. Nashville: Abingdon Press, 1983.

Lewis, C. S. *Surprised by Joy*. New York: Harcourt, Brace and Company, 1955.

Ortberg, John. *Love Beyond Reason*. Grand Rapids: Zondervan, 1998.

Peck, Scott. *Gifts for the Journey*. San Francisco: HarperCollins, 1995.

CHAPTER SEVEN

Grace-Filled:
Dealing with Sin

I believe there is a general sentiment that sin is still with us, by us, and in us—somewhere.
   —Karl Menninger, Whatever Became of Sin? *p. 17*

Like just about everyone else, I've discovered the wonders of life on the Internet, with all those E-mail messages flying back and forth around the planet. I keep wondering, *When I click on "delete," where does all that stuff go?*

Pulling up my E-mail one morning, I discovered a disturbing warning about the dangers of a vicious computer virus that could enter my computer through a message with the unlikely title of "Good Times." The warning declared that by receiving that message, a virus would be let loose that could destroy everything in my computer's hard drive. I sent a panic-stricken message to a friendly computer expert, who assured me that it was a hoax. There was no "Good Times" virus, he said, and I probably didn't need to worry about losing all of the sermons stored on my hard drive, but he hoped that I knew enough to back up or copy all of my files anyway.

The "Good Times" computer virus was a hoax, but it got my attention. Lo and behold, the time came when an unknown, unnamed virus hit my computer. I was in Boston. When I booted up my computer and went online to check my office E-mail, an insidious little smiling face popped up and multiplied itself across the laptop screen. I immediately shut down the computer and called our all-knowing church administrator. She made it clear that under no circumstances could I boot up the computer again or it could destroy the entire hard drive. For the rest of the trip, every time I put my computer case on my shoulder, I knew that it contained a dangerous virus that had the capability of destroying our entire system. There was nothing I could do to repair it until I turned it over to the computer-repair folk who could purge that virus.

Since that time, the memory of that experience has worked its way into my thinking as a contemporary analogy to the reality of human sin. In his letter to the Romans, Paul wrote: "Sin came into the world through one man, and death came through sin, and so death spread to all because all have sinned" (Rom. 5:12). Had Paul been writing to a computer-oriented culture, he might have said, "One person downloaded the virus of sin into the human network, and it spread throughout the entire system."

An online friend told me that his computer system had been down for three days. He spent long hours trying to find the problem. He finally discovered that one comma was out of place in the program. He said, "I spent three days trying to fix everything except the real problem." Soul-pilgrims on a journey to the center of the faith are clear-eyed realists about the real problem in the human network. The Bible calls it sin. It is the destructive virus that affects the entire system.

There ain't gonna be no whiskey; there ain't gonna be no gin;
There ain't gonna be no highball to put the whiskey in;
There ain't gonna be no cigarettes to make folks pale and thin;
But you can't take away the tendency to sin, sin, sin.
—*Vaughn Miller, 1919, quoted in the* New York
Public Library Book of 20th Century Quotations, *p. 177*

When the apostle Paul said that "sin came into the world through one man," he was referring to Adam, the Old Testament archetype of our humanity. Contrary to popular opinion, the story of "the Fall" in Genesis 3 has nothing to do with apples, little to do with snakes, and even less to do with some of the bad jokes and dubious theology that have evolved from it. Because it was first passed on by oral tradition, it helps to read the story aloud.

There was a serpent, and the serpent was more crafty than any other animal that the LORD God had made, and he said to the woman, "Sssssssssssss . . . Did God say you shall not eat from any tree in the garden?" And the woman said to the serpent, "We may eat the fruit of the trees of the garden, but God said, 'You shall not eat the fruit of the tree that is in the middle of the garden, nor shall you touch it, or you shall die!' " But the serpent said to the woman, "Sssssssssssss . . . You shall not die, for God knows that when you eat of it, your eyes will be opened and you will be like God! Sssssssssssss." (Gen. 3:1-5, adapted, with sound effects added!)

 The Bible is clear that the root cause of sin is our arrogant desire to be like God—to have life our way without regard to anything larger than our own self-interest, to be totally self-sufficient, with no need for anyone or anything else. It grows out of a passionate longing to organize all of life around our self-satisfying desires and our inordinate lust for power, with no accountability to the purpose of the Creator and no responsibility to the rest of the creation. The serpent's temptation was "you shall be like God"—and Adam and Eve fell for it. Sin came into the world like a destructive virus. And sin spread, affecting the whole creation.

On February 22, 1972, the most perfect baby that had ever been born arrived at Central Baptist Hospital in Lexington, Kentucky. I should know—I'm her father! I remember driving through town thinking to myself, "Look at all these people! They're still walking around as if nothing has happened! The stoplights are still changing as if this were just another day!" I was sure that Carrie Lynn was the most beautiful little girl in the history of the human race until Deborah Jeanne arrived two years later, and then we had both of them!

But something happened to those perfect little girls. I soon discovered that I didn't need to teach them to be selfish. I didn't need to teach them how to sin. It came as a part of their natural human instincts. Even my perfect little girls were infected.

Some doctrinal theories declare that sin is passed on genetically. But the apostle Paul never attempted an explanation of *how* sin spreads; he simply knew *that* it spreads, with the result that "all [of us] have sinned." The sin of Adam and Eve is not just an ancient religious tale from the dusty pages of the book of Genesis. It is your story and mine. All of us are infected. It is the biblical diagnosis of our fundamental human ailment. It is a part of the warp and woof of our common history.

Sin spreads not only through our personal lives and individual choices but also through the social structures, political institutions, and power systems of our world. In his letter to the Ephesians, Paul declared that "our struggle is not against enemies of blood and flesh, but against the rulers, against the authorities, against the cosmic powers of this present darkness, against the spiritual forces of evil" (Eph. 6:12). The viruses of racism, violence, economic exploitation, sexual perversion and abuse, political injustice, and environmental destruction point to systemic sin that is more than merely the sum total of the sinful choices of individual persons. The power of sin takes on a life of its own and often takes subtle control of the very people who try to control it.

New Testament scholar Walter Wink has invested most of his career in studying the biblical view of power. He describes "the actual spirituality of systems and structures that have betrayed their divine vocations . . . what happens when an entire network of Powers becomes integrated around idolatrous values . . . the impersonal spiritual realities at the center of institutional life" (*Engaging the Powers*, pp. 8-9). His vision of the spiritual nature of power within social structures and cultural systems helps explain why it is so difficult for good people with good intentions to change the direction and unintended destructive effects of the organizations and cultures within which they live.

I am a member of the high-school class of 1965, a child of the idealism of the early 1960s. My adolescent values were shaped in the days of "the new frontier" and nurtured in an era of high hopes for cultural change. A huge percentage of my peers actually believed that the civil rights movement could end racism, that the peace movement could stop war, that "the great society" would end poverty, and that we would see "the dawning of the Age of Aquarius." But much of that social idealism was blown to smithereens with the deaths of John and Robert Kennedy and Martin Luther King, Jr., the publishing of "the Pentagon papers," and the whole sad saga that began with a botched break-in at Watergate. The hopes for change were dashed on the rocks in the realization of the intransigence of power and the insidious influence of evil. Nearly forty years later, about the only folk left with much idealism about cultural change are those whose hopes were rooted in religious faith—specifically, those who continue to believe in Jesus' vision of the kingdom of God coming on earth as it is in heaven. But that kingdom-idealism has been tempered by a far more realistic understanding of the systemic power of sin.

We are speaking now of a deeper evil—a layer of sludge beneath the murky waters that can be characterized only as a hellish hatred of the light, of truth, of kindness and compassion, a brute lust for annihilation. It is the sedimentation of thousands of years of human choices for evil (not wrong *choices merely, but actual choices for evil) . . . the spirituality of evil.*
—*Walter Wink*, Engaging the Powers, *p. 69*

But Paul did not write his Epistle to the Romans merely to report how bad sin is. He wrote it to declare how good God's grace is! The Epistle announces the good news: "But the free gift is not like the trespass" (Rom. 5:15). Paul was drawing the contrast between Adam and Jesus in cosmic terms. In Adam's story, one person's disobedience to God's loving purpose unleashed the virus of sin that led to death. In Jesus' story, one man's obedience to the redemptive, costly, loving will of God released the power of God's grace that leads to life.

> The free gift is not like the trespass. For if the many died through the one man's trespass, much more surely have the grace of God and the free gift in the grace of the one man, Jesus Christ, abounded for the many. And the free gift is not like the effect of the one man's sin. For the judgment following one trespass brought condemnation. (Rom. 5:15-16*a*)

Sin always leads to death. When we give in to the power of sin, we set ourselves on a path that ultimately condemns us to our own self-destruction, as well as the destruction of others.

> . . . but the free gift following many trespasses brings justification. If, because of the one man's trespass, death exercised dominion through that one, much more surely will those who receive the

abundance of grace and the free gift of righteousness exercise dominion in life through the one man, Jesus Christ.

Therefore, just as one man's trespass led to condemnation for all, so one man's act of righteousness leads to justification and life for all. For just as by the one man's disobedience the many were made sinners, so by the one man's obedience the many will be made righteous. . . . Just as sin exercised dominion in death, so grace might also exercise dominion through justification leading to eternal life through Jesus Christ our Lord. (Rom. 5:16*b*-21)

Just as the "bad news" virus of sin spread throughout human existence, so the "good news" of God's grace spreads health and wholeness through human history, bringing new life for all. Paul's vision is not unlike the way our computer-savvy church administrator installed a virus-cleaning program that swept through the entire network and corrected what the virus had messed up.

The New Testament parallel to the Genesis story of Adam's temptation in the garden is the Gospel account of Jesus' temptation in the wilderness. The same tempter came to Jesus and said, "*Sssssssssssss* . . . If you are the Son of God, command these stones to become loaves of bread" (Matt. 4:3, adapted). The temptation was clear: *Go ahead, Jesus, satisfy yourself! Use your God-given gift for your own selfish gratification!*

But [Jesus] answered, "It is written, 'One does not live by bread alone, but by every word that comes from the mouth of God.'"

Then the devil took him to the holy city and placed him on the pinnacle of the temple, saying to him, "*Ssssssssssssss* . . . If you are the Son of God, throw yourself down; for it is written, 'He will command his angels concerning you,' and 'On their hands they will bear you up, so that you will not dash your foot against a stone.'"

Come on, Jesus! Use some of your divine, God-given power to take care of yourself!

Jesus said to him, "Again it is written, 'Do not put the Lord your God to the test.'"

Again, the devil took him to a very high mountain and showed him all the kingdoms of the world and their splendor; and he said to him, "*Sssssssssssss* . . . All these I will give you, if you will fall down and worship me."

Go ahead, Jesus. Draw attention to yourself. Set yourself up on your own throne! You have it in your power to be like God!

Jesus said to him, "Away with you, Satan! for it is written, 'Worship the Lord your God, and serve only him.' " (Matt. 4:1-10, adapted)

In the wilderness, Jesus faced the same temptations Adam and Eve faced in the garden and the same temptations that confront each of us every day. The transforming hinge of redemptive history swings on Jesus' refusal to use the power of God to satisfy his own self-centered desires. Rather, he surrendered himself to the cross in obedience to the self-giving love and purpose of God.

Jesus' temptation did not end in the wilderness. The tempter came again at the end of Jesus' life. On the night before he died, Jesus was tempted to save himself by finding some way to avoid going to the cross. Again denying his own self-interest, he offered himself for the fulfillment of the purpose of the self-giving love of God when he prayed, "My Father, if it is possible, let this cup pass from me; yet not what I want but what you want" (see Matt. 26:36-39).

Jesus at his crucifixion neither fights the darkness nor flees under cover of it, but goes with it, goes into it. He enters the darkness, freely, voluntarily. . . . The massive forces arrayed in opposition to the truth are revealed to be puny over against the force of a free human being.
—*Walter Wink,* Engaging the Powers, *p. 141*

Paul declared that Jesus' act of obedience released the abundance of God's grace for the whole of creation. The idea was so overpowering that Paul could not find language big enough to describe it. In Romans 5:20 he used a Greek expression for which there is no direct English equivalent. The Greek verb is repeated, and a superlative is added the second time around. Translators have attempted to capture something of the power of that verb in several ways:

King James Version: "Where sin abounded, grace did much more abound."

New English Bible: "Where sin was thus multiplied, grace immeasurably exceeded it."

J. B. Phillips: "Though sin is shown to be wide and deep, thank God his grace is wider and deeper still!"

Paul does not hold the alternatives of human sin and God's grace in any sort of equal balance. Adam's puny act of self-centered sin is totally outweighed by the infinite love and grace revealed in the cross of Jesus Christ. The result is that we cannot "out-sin" the love and grace of God! It is bigger and deeper than all our sin. That's why it is big enough to save us!

So the apostle places two alternative realities before us: Adam's act of self-oriented disobedience on one side, Jesus' act of self-giving obedience on the other. Sin on one side of the scale, grace outweighing it on the other. Death on one hand, life on the other. And we are called to choose. We can choose to turn the central part of our being either in the direction of Adam and sin, which results in death, or in the direction of the free gift of God's grace in Jesus Christ, which brings life. We can choose, within the sin-infected systems of our world, to surrender ourselves to their controlling powers or to model the redemptive nonviolence of Jesus' death on the cross. We can continue to allow our lives and our world to be contaminated with the self-destructive power of sin, or we can allow the new life of the Resurrection to spread like a healing antidote through the rest of the system.

[Christ] came to this world and became a man in order to spread to other men the kind of life He has—by what I call "good infection." Every Christian is to become a little Christ. The whole purpose of becoming a Christian is simply nothing else.

—C. S. *Lewis*, Mere Christianity, *p. 154*

I received an E-mail from a man who ended up in our church by accident. He was looking for another meeting when he stepped into a room where I was leading our "Fresh Start" group for people who are considering the Christian faith for the first time. The group welcomed him so warmly that he stayed. He showed up in worship the next Sunday, joined a Disciple Bible Study group, and began to turn his life in a new direction. His letter described the process by which God's grace became a reality for him:

> I found at Hyde Park a church which portrayed a God which held out his hand and said, "I have a gift of a wonderful life for you. It will have sorrow and stress. But the gift I have to give to you will give you the inner peace to survive all that trauma with a true happiness in your heart. The gift will give you strength when you need it, let you laugh when you need it, will let you love life, love yourself and others. It will let you appreciate every person, though you may not like them. It will be so wonderful that you will actively seek it out and strive to live with the gift at all times. Because once you lose it, you will fall back into a world of hostility, anger, frustration, and rage. I only have one requirement for you. YOU HAVE TO ASK FOR IT FROM ME. I AM THE ONLY ONE WHO CAN GIVE IT TO YOU." As a result, I have been actively seeking the gift ever since.

I have watched in amazement as this man has turned the central part of his being in the direction of new life in Christ; along the way, that life has spread through his attitudes, relationships, priorities, and career. Grace, once received in Jesus Christ, spreads!

How to Deal with Sin

1. What comes to your mind when you hear the word *sin*? Explain.

2. How do you experience the power of temptation? How can you identify with Jesus' temptations in the wilderness?

3. How does sin spread? How have you experienced the systemic powers of evil?

4. What is your understanding of what Jesus did at the cross? How does it transform your understanding of the power of evil?

5. Think about the ordinary choices of your life. What will it mean for you to choose to turn the central part of your life toward Adam/sin/death or Christ/grace/life?

6. How have you discovered the "super-abounding" grace of God in your life?

Resources for Dealing with Sin

Lewis, C. S. *The Screwtape Letters*. New York: Macmillan, 1961.
———. *Mere Christianity*. New York: Macmillan, 1952.
Lucado, Max. *He Chose the Nails: What God Did to Win Your Heart*. Waco: Word, 2000.
McCullough, Donald W. *The Trivialization of God: The Dangerous Illusion of a Manageable Deity*. Colorado Springs: Navpress, 1995.
Menninger, Karl. *Whatever Became of Sin?* New York: Hawthorn, 1973.
Plantinga, Cornelius. *Not the Way It's Supposed to Be*. Grand Rapids: Eerdmans, 1995.
Wink, Walter. *Engaging the Powers: Discernment and Resistance in a World of Domination*. Minneapolis: Fortress Press, 1992.
Yancey, Philip. *What's So Amazing About Grace?* Grand Rapids: Zondervan, 1997.

CHAPTER EIGHT

Soul-Strengthened: Facing Up to Suffering

To be painlessly happy, and to conquer every form of suffering,
is part of the dream of modern society. But since the dream is
unattainable, people anesthetize pain, and suppress suffering,
and by so doing rob themselves of the passion for life.
        —*Jürgen Moltmann,* The Way of Jesus Christ, *p. 151*

I used to think it took too long for Hamlet to die. I thought Shakespeare made the play's final scene go on far too long, with too many interminable lines to deliver. But then I listened to the kids from Columbine High School in Littleton, Colorado, talk about their teacher and coach who was shot during the bloody rampage of violence that hit their school in the spring of 1999. For three hours they waited with him, worked to stop the bleeding from his wounds, and listened to him as he talked about his family. Eventually, as the students escaped to safety, their teacher died. Watching the students' faces and listening to their words in interviews, I remembered some of Hamlet's closing lines:

> If thou didst ever hold me in thy heart,
> Absent thee from felicity awhile,
> And in this harsh world draw thy breath in pain
> To tell my story. (Act 5, scene 2)

And so in this harsh world, in the aftermath of the violence in Littleton and a similar attack at Heritage High School in Atlanta, we spent the last spring and summer of the millennium drawing our breath in pain to hear them tell their stories. Absent from felicity for a while, we saw the tear-stained faces, the bleeding bodies. The television images that flooded our living rooms reminded us of the incomprehensible cost of evil and of this world's mad addiction to violence.

The violence was not confined to the United States. The death and destruction in Littleton brought the reality of that spring's death and destruction in Yugoslavia onto the soil of our lives. I found it interesting that when we heard the reports of death in Kosovo it was called "genocide," but when we heard reports of death in Belgrade, we called it "collateral damage." Now there's a demonic term right out of the pit of hell, if ever there was one. Do you know what "collateral damage" is to God? "Collateral damage" means the death of real people, with real names and real stories to tell—just as real as the kids who died at Columbine High.

In this harsh world we draw our breath in pain to tell the stories of suffering. But the suffering extends beyond the big news stories that capture the headlines. Our very anonymous lives are filled with anonymous-but-no-less-painful stories of loss, disappointment, suffering, and death, stories that will never be reported on CNN. They are our stories—stories of the suffering that touches every last one of us.

I am convinced that where life is beginning and where life is ending is holy ground. The knowledge of the imminence of death is a gift that sets us on holy ground. Or perhaps it is more accurate to say it is the gift of awareness of the holy ground on which we are always standing.
    —hospice worker Bettye Jo Bell, quoted in Context, May 15, 1989, p. 5

If we tell the truth, we must confess that suffering tests our faith. The apostle Peter compared our experience of suffering to the way gold is tested in the fire to measure its worth: "In this you rejoice, even if now for a little while you have had to suffer various trials, so that the genuineness of your faith—being more precious than gold that, though perishable, is tested by fire—may be found to result in praise and glory and honor when Jesus Christ is revealed" (1 Pet. 1:6).

Nothing tests our faith, nothing plunges us more deeply into the center of our relationship with God, nothing plumbs the depth of our souls, no single issue causes more theological and spiritual confusion than the issue of suffering. How can we believe in a good God in an evil world? How can we trust the love of God when we experience so much pain? Where is the center that will hold in the middle of the chaotic suffering of the world?

Hours after the rampage at Columbine High, I took a call from a news reporter at one of the local TV stations. She was checking in to see what a pastor might have to say about the tragedy. In the process of the conversation, I suggested that she be careful about who she listened to. I told her that for me the only thing worse than some of the stories coming out of Littleton would be the abysmal theology some religious folk would wrap around them.

I knew that some well-intended, faithful people would be quick to say, "God had a reason for this." This is one of the most common pieces of American folk heresy I know. It makes me want to ask, "What kind of god do you believe in, for God's sake?" I told her that if I thought God had a causative, purposeful hand in what happened in Littleton, if I thought God had specifically chosen which kids would live and which would die, then I thought I would rather be an atheist.

Or, some sensitive person would attempt to soften the grief of a brokenhearted parent by saying, "God must have needed another angel in heaven." When I hear this, a rebellious part of me wants to shout, "To hell with angels!" From a biblical standpoint, some of the shallow theology that gets wrapped around human suffering in the name of religion is enough to defame the name of God. Some of it leaves us with a god who is neither fit to love nor worthy of trust. Behind the layers of syrupy sentimentality there lurks a heartless god who would be the sinister contradiction of the character of the God revealed in Jesus Christ.

Recognizing the necessity for suffering I have tried to make of it a virtue. If only to save myself from bitterness, I have attempted to see my personal ordeals as an opportunity to transform myself and heal the people. . . . I have lived these last few years with the conviction that unearned suffering is redemptive.

—*Martin Luther King Jr.*, A Testament of Hope, *p. 41*

If we use the First Epistle of Peter as a signpost for a journey to the soul-strengthening center of our faith, we are confronted with two formative issues. First, the question is not *if* we will face suffering, but *when* we will face it.

The New Testament never promises that faith in the risen Christ will guarantee supernatural immunity from the pain and suffering of this very real and very dangerous world. There are forms of spirituality that offer an escape hatch from suffering, but none of them are centered in the cross. The Bible takes human suffering as a basic assumption. It can happen to any of us. I heard about a rabbi who said that expecting the world to treat us fairly because we are good people is like expecting a bull not to charge because we are vegetarian. That's not pessimism; it's just the reality of life in a harsh and broken world. It can happen to any of us.

But the gospel goes a step further. Peter tied human suffering directly to the suffering of Jesus. Our Lord went to the cross, he said, and we will too.

> For it is a credit to you if, being aware of God, you endure pain while suffering unjustly. If you endure when you are beaten for doing wrong, what credit is that? But if you endure when you do right and suffer for it, you have God's approval. For to this you have been called, because Christ also suffered for you, leaving you an example, so that you should follow in his steps.
> "He committed no sin,
>   and no deceit was found in his mouth."
> When he was abused, he did not return abuse; when he suffered, he did not threaten; but he entrusted himself to the one who judges justly. He himself bore our sins in his body on the cross, so that, free from sins, we might live for righteousness; by his wounds you have been healed. (1 Pet. 2:19-24)

The New Testament declares that the more faithfully we follow the will and way of Jesus, the more we can expect to experience the pain and suffering of a hostile world. The more deeply we love, the more deeply we feel the pain of others. The closer we are to the heart of God, the more our hearts will be broken by the things that break the heart of God. Every journey to the center of the faith will ultimately lead to a cross. We need not be surprised by it. The question is not *if* we will experience suffering, but *when*.

❖

There are some who still find the cross a stumbling block, and others consider it foolishness, but I am more convinced than ever before that it is the power of God unto social and individual salvation.
　　　　　—*Martin Luther King Jr.*, A Testament of Hope, *p. 42*

❖

The second formative question, both biblically and experientially, is not *why* we face suffering, but *how* we face it. When bad things happen we naturally ask *Why?* But we'd better watch out. Most of the time, if we honestly search for the answer, it may come right back to point at us.

Why conflict in Yugoslavia? Just read the history. The ethnic and political conflict that tears nations into warring factions isn't God's doing. It is the result of generations of inbred hatred. It is the result of powerful nations carving up boundaries as the spoils of military victory. It is the consequence of jingoistic pride, national arrogance, and sheer stupidity. It is because we who hold the power of military might continue to be tricked by the demonic lie that we can accomplish peace and justice by the means of war. It is because we do not really believe that the way of Jesus represents the rule of God carved into human history. God isn't on the hook for a huge amount of the suffering in this world—*we* are.

Why death and destruction at a high school in Colorado? Why school shootings in Kentucky, Arkansas, and Georgia? Why gunshots at a Jewish community center in California? Just look around. Look at our cultural addiction to violence. Look at the images that saturate our movie and television screens with death. Look at the way we condition kids to think that the only way to resolve conflict is with force. Look at the way we raise boys in this culture. Have you noticed that practically none of these school shootings has been committed by a girl? Should this not raise some questions about the way we are "raising Cain" in this culture?

Look at the amount of money we spend arming ourselves in comparison to the amount of money we spend educating our children. Look at our immoral addiction to guns. I cannot figure out why it is reasonable to require a license to drive a car, but it is unreasonable to require a license to shoot an AK-47. Why do we so easily accept a nation in which we have more guns than we have citizens?

Careful readers are often surprised to discover that the Bible never spends much time asking or attempting to answer the question *Why?* When it does—in the book of Job—the answer ends in mystery. Job's friends give him all the wrong answers. They are the same wrong answers our friends usually give us. Some of them sound good, but they never hold up in the storm. When God finally gets to put in a divine word, the voice of God speaks with soaring Hebrew satire:

> "Where were you when I laid the foundation of the earth?
>   Tell me, if you have understanding.
> Who determined its measurements—surely you know!
>   Or who stretched the line upon it?
> On what were its bases sunk,
>   or who laid its cornerstone
> when the morning stars sang together
>   and all the heavenly beings shouted for joy?" (Job 38:4-7)

The Bible is not concerned with *why* we face suffering, except to the degree that we see much of the suffering inflicted on the human family as the result of our human rebellion against the will of God. But the Bible is very concerned about *how* we face suffering. The New Testament writers celebrate the transforming assurance that the love and grace of God have already won the victory over suffering and death in the resurrection of Jesus Christ.

God wanted to liberate us, not by removing suffering from us, but by sharing it with us.
      —Henri Nouwen, Letters to Marc About Jesus, *p. 31*

In my ministry I've watched all sorts of people go through all sorts of pain, loss, tragedy, and death. I've observed that the difference between them is not whether they suffer, but how they face it. The difference is not the amount of suffering, but the depth of the spiritual and personal resources they bring to it.

I have a very pragmatic reason for developing a growing,

mature, profoundly biblical relationship with God: I know that
sooner or later I will need the strength it brings. Sooner or later, I
will walk through the valley of the shadow. I've been there before;
I'll be there again. Sooner or later, I will confront the awesome
power of pain, hurt, suffering, or loss. The only question is
whether I will have developed the spiritual resources to confront it
and not be destroyed by it. Like the wise man in Jesus' parable,
will I have built the house of my soul on a strong enough foundation to withstand the storm?

> "Everyone then who hears these words of mine and acts on them
> will be like a wise man who built his house on rock. The rain fell,
> the floods came, and the winds blew and beat on that house, but it
> did not fall, because it had been founded on rock. And everyone
> who hears these words of mine and does not act on them will be like
> a foolish man who built his house on sand. The rain fell, and the
> floods came, and the winds blew and beat against that house, and it
> fell—and great was its fall!" (Matt. 7:24-27)

The First Epistle of Peter was addressed to ethnic refugees, political exiles, and ordinary slaves who were experiencing the full
weight of unjust suffering. The writer of this letter reminded them
of the risen Christ and called them to hold on to the hope that
belonged to them because of the Resurrection. If we allow these
words to speak to us, we will find some very practical guidance in
how to face suffering.

Number one: Follow Jesus.

> For to this you have been called, because Christ also suffered for
> you, leaving you an example, so that you should follow in his steps.
> (1 Pet. 2:21)

The apostle calls us to move into human suffering in the same
spirit and with the same obedience with which Jesus went to the
cross. The only way I know to do that is to get to know Jesus' story
so well that we begin to respond to the pain and suffering of this
world the way Jesus responded to the suffering in his life. You can
hear the depth of that challenge in the fourth chapter of the Epistle:
"Since therefore Christ suffered in the flesh, arm yourselves also

with the same intention . . . so as to live for the rest of your earthly life no longer by human desires but by the will of God" (1 Pet. 4:1-2).

Number two: Resist evil. Peter calls us to build up the moral and spiritual steel in our souls.

> Discipline yourselves, keep alert. Like a roaring lion your adversary the devil prowls around, looking for someone to devour. Resist him, steadfast in your faith. (1 Pet. 5:8)

> Do not fear what they fear, and do not be intimidated, but in your hearts sanctify Christ as Lord. Always be ready to make your defense to anyone who demands from you an accounting for the hope that is in you; yet do it with gentleness and reverence. (1 Pet. 3:14-16)

There's no copping out on the reality of evil in this harsh world, but we are called to confront it, not in our own power, but in the power of the Spirit of God.

Number three: Continue to do good.

> Therefore, let those suffering in accordance with God's will entrust themselves to a faithful Creator, while continuing to do good. (1 Pet. 4:19)

One of the insidious effects of the massive evil and suffering of our world is that it tends to intimidate and immobilize us. We begin to say, "What can I do? What difference does my little contribution to goodness make in the face of such massive evil?" Peter says, "Continue to do good." Keep on doing whatever you can. Touch life where you can touch it. Heal brokenness where you can heal it. Model the new life of the kingdom of God in every way you can. In the tradition of John Wesley, we are challenged to do all the good we can, by all the means we can, for as long as we can.

Number four: Share your suffering.

> Finally, all of you, have unity of spirit, sympathy, love for one another, a tender heart, and a humble mind. (1 Pet. 3:8)

In the Body of Christ, no one needs to suffer alone. We are called to share each other's suffering. Both of our daughters experienced the loss of high-school friends in car accidents. As we were going through the grief process, I was amazed to discover that my daughters had received a very special gift. Because of my role as a pastor, they had seen and experienced death within the church family. They had heard us talk about people who were hurting. They had been to funeral services in the church. Because they had shared the experience of suffering, we suddenly discovered that they had inner resources to face those losses that many of the other kids did not have. It was the kind of inner strength that comes through shared suffering.

Number five: Search for joy.

The most amazing thing about the First Epistle of Peter is that it is so full of joy. Given the oppressive conditions under which its recipients were suffering, the letter could have been a somber, serious, heavy word. But from beginning to end, the letter reverberates with joy.

> In this you rejoice, even if now for a little while you have had to suffer various trials, so that the genuineness of your faith—being more precious than gold that, though perishable, is tested by fire—may be found to result in praise and glory and honor when Jesus Christ is revealed. Although you have not seen him, you love him; and even though you do not see him now, you believe in him and rejoice with an indescribable and glorious joy, for you are receiving the outcome of your faith, the salvation of your souls. (1 Pet. 1:6-9)

The writer is not talking about happiness as the world defines it, happiness that is dependent on circumstances. The word is *joy*—deep, inner, resilient, irrepressible joy that flows from the same place as tears. Joy that is not dependent on present circumstances, but is deeply rooted in the power of the risen Christ. It's the kind of faith that every minute claims the gift of joy in the midst of suffering and hangs on to it as if life depended on it.

Number six: Trust God.

Therefore, let those suffering in accordance with God's will entrust themselves to a faithful Creator. (1 Pet. 4:19)

After you have suffered for a little while, the God of all grace, who has called you to his eternal glory in Christ, will himself restore, support, strengthen, and establish you. To him be the power forever and ever. Amen. (1 Pet. 5:10)

Do you want to know where the real power is in this world? It is the power of God's love at the cross that was vindicated in the Resurrection. In the face of suffering, we continue to believe that love is ultimately stronger than hate. Peace is ultimately stronger than conflict. Life is ultimately stronger than death. We can trust the God who has called us in Christ to restore, support, strengthen, and uphold us.

We draw our breath in pain to tell the stories. Human suffering is a very real part of the very real world in which we live. But we draw our spiritual breath from a deeper, stronger, and more powerful place. We draw our breath from the power of the life-giving God who raised Jesus Christ from the dead.

My strength is not in me, but in him, who when he calls me to do a thing also gives the power to do that thing. It is not my ability, but my response to his ability. It isn't what happens to us that matters, but what we do with what happens to us that counts. . . . Everything furthers those who follow Christ.

—*E. Stanley Jones,* The Divine Yes, *pp. 127-28*

How to Strengthen the Soul

1. Read what First Peter has to say about suffering (1 Pet. 1:3-9; 2:19-25; 3:8-22; 4:12-19; 5:6-11). Imagine that you were among the first recipients of this letter. How do these words make you feel? How do they speak to your experience of suffering?

2. How does this chapter affect your understanding of God and suffering?

3. Walk through the six words of guidance from First Peter for how to face suffering, as outlined in this chapter. How would following these steps help you personally to deal with suffering?

4. When have you experienced suffering? How did you respond? What difference did your faith make for your experience?

Resources for Strengthening the Soul

Jones, E. Stanley. *The Divine Yes*. Nashville: Abingdon Press, 1975.

King, Martin Luther, Jr. *A Testament of Hope: The Essential Writings and Speeches of Martin Luther King, Jr.*, edited by James M. Washington. New York: HarperSanFrancisco, 1986.

Moltmann, Jürgen. *The Way of Jesus Christ: Christology in Messianic Dimensions*. Minneapolis: Fortress Press, 1993.

Norris, Kathleen. *Amazing Grace: A Vocabulary of Faith*. New York: Riverhead Books, 1998.

Nouwen, Henri J. M. *Letters to Marc About Jesus*. New York: Harper & Row, 1988.

Price, Reynolds. *Letter to a Man in the Fire*. New York: Scribner, 1999.

Wuellner, Flora Slosson. *Feed My Shepherds: Spiritual Healing and Renewal for Those in Christian Leadership*. Nashville: Upper Room, 1998.

CHAPTER NINE

Community-Connected: Making New Connections

The center of our harmony and of our unity is Jesus Christ. . . . .
If I ask, "What do you believe?" we will go apart, no two believ-
ing exactly alike. If I ask, "Whom do you trust?" we will come
together, one name upon our lips, one loyalty in our hearts. . . .
Outside him . . . all things fly apart. . . . Jesus Christ, and Jesus
Christ alone, is the center of our unity.
　　　　　　　—E. Stanley Jones, Song of Ascents, *pp. 279, 284*

*V*oid If Detached. I had seen these words on theater tickets, travel vouchers, and theme-park passes. They usually appear just above the perforation where the attendant tears the stub you keep from the part he takes as you go through the turnstiles. I knew that these words meant that one part of the ticket separated from the other would render the entire ticket void, ineffective, and useless. *Void If Detached* means that one part is incapable of accomplishing its intended purpose without the other.

I was making my way through the New Testament Letter to the Hebrews. I knew that in the eleventh chapter the writer takes the readers on a walking tour of the "biblical hall of fame." I had taken the tour before. All the heroes of the Old Testament are there: Abraham and Sarah, Isaac, Moses, Gideon, David, and more. But I was surprised by what the guide said at the end of the tour: "Yet all these, though they were commended for their faith, did not receive what was promised, since God had provided something better so that they would not, apart from us, be made perfect" (Heb. 11:39).

What a mind-stretching assertion! The writer claims that even the witness of the greatest saints is incomplete if they are cut off from the people of faith in every age. These words in the Letter to the Hebrews gave a whole new meaning to the phrase *Void If Detached*.

Individual Christianity is a self-contradiction! Unless there is a sense of "one another" there is no sense of the Living Christ.
—Elton Trueblood, The Future of the Christian
(New York: Harper & Row, 1971), p. 22

The New Testament vision of life centered in Christ is persistently communal. Life in Christ is always life in connection with others. Biblically speaking, "solitary salvation" is an oxymoron. It is a contradiction in terms. Throughout the Old Testament, living by faith means being a part of God's community of the covenant people in the line of Abraham and Sarah. In the New Testament, salvation—our new relationship with God—means becoming a part of the "new creation" in the Body of Christ. When we are "born again," we are born into a family with brothers and sisters whom we do not choose. They are given to us in the love of God. Being "saved" does not mean holding a solitary ticket for a solo flight to heaven. It means becoming a part of the Body of Christ, living on earth in ways that are consistent with the rule of God that is already fulfilled in heaven.

My own vision of the Christian life was forever changed when I heard E. Stanley Jones say, "Everyone who belongs to Christ belongs to everyone who belongs to Christ" (*A Song of Ascents*, p. 284). While his affirmation runs across the grain of our individualism, it touches one of the persistent soul-needs of our culture today: we are searching for our place to belong.

niche (nich), n., v., niched, niching.—n. 1 a recess or hollow in a wall, as for a statue or vase. 2 Figurative. a suitable place or position; place for which a person is suited. 3 Ecology. the function of an organism within a community
—The World Book Dictionary
(Chicago: Doubleday, 1984), p. 1402

There was a time when everyone seemed to "know their place" in this society. The boundaries were clear. The boxes were neatly labeled. We all knew where we belonged. But those days are gone. While the world has become smaller, it has also become infinitely more complex and amazingly diverse. The old human file cabinets simply do not fit anymore. The result is that each of us is searching for our "niche," our place to belong.

The heart longing for a place to belong was captured in the theme song of one of the most popular TV shows of all time. A major segment of the population structured their week around the moment when a wistful voice asked if we wouldn't like to get away to a place where everybody knows our name. Millions of people tuned into *Cheers* not just because it was funny, but because it touched a deep nerve within us. We have a profound need to find a place to belong, a place where we are known, a place where we know that our stool is waiting and our friends will call us by name.

With the passing of *Cheers*, American audiences turned to *Seinfeld* and *Friends*. Both shows were built around the close relationships the characters shared with one another. My own conviction is that these shows were popular not because people *have* these kinds of relationships, but because they *desire* them so deeply. Unfortunately, such shows also often demonstrate how unbelievably shallow and self-centered most relationships in our culture seem to be these days, as well as our contemporary addiction to radical self-centeredness. The final episode of *Seinfeld* left the characters imprisoned in their own self-absorption. But even in its weakness, the series demonstrated our hunger for relationships.

A "Gen-X" forum sponsored by Leadership Network drew over two hundred leaders of ministry with the twenty-something generation to Colorado Springs in 1996. Defining the spiritual needs of the "baby-buster" generation, Kevin Ford said, "We [Xers] need help connecting. . . . Our families were supposed to teach us how to interact, how to connect, but many were unhealthy and some of us never learned how" (*Netfax*, March 18, 1996).

The New Testament offers a model of Christian community that speaks directly to our deepest longing to belong. It began the day Jesus chose a dozen very unexceptional people to be his disciples. He called them by name, taught them, trained them, and sent them out as the agents of the reign of God (see Matt. 10:1-15). In some of his last words to them before his death, Jesus defined the intimate nature of their relationship:

> "You are my friends if you do what I command you. I do not call you servants any longer, because the servant does not know what the master is doing; but I have called you friends, because I have made known to you everything that I have heard from my Father." (John 15:14-15)

Jesus set the example for relationships in which everyone—even Judas, who betrayed him—found their niche in the kingdom-shaped life of the people of God.

Nearly two decades ago I was invited to lead a retreat on spiritual discipline for some pastors in another part of the state. By the time that retreat was over, I was there not as a leader but as a participant in what has become one of the most formative relationships of my life. Nine of us gather twice a year for laughter, study, self-revelation, and prayer. We've encouraged one another in difficult times, celebrated with one another in times of joy, and supported one another in making difficult choices. We have experienced the real presence of the living Christ through the sacrament of friendship. It has been a part of God's saving work in each of our lives.

Jesus taught a faith that cannot be lived outside a web of relationships, some strands of which tear away at you while also lifting you upright. In biblical ways of thinking, you cannot discover who you are, much less become who you are, without friends.
—Leonard I. Sweet, The Jesus Prescription for a Healthy Life
(Nashville: Abingdon Press, 1996), p. 34

The pattern of communal faith that Jesus modeled with the disciples became the pattern for the early church in the book of Acts. Luke describes two indispensable elements in their life together. One was the gathered congregation. Except for times when persecution drove them underground, all the believers—sometimes thousands of them—gathered to hear the apostles' preaching, to celebrate their faith in the risen Christ, and to welcome new persons into the Christian community. The second indispensable element was the "house church," small gatherings of disciples in which the followers of Jesus studied together and cared for one another, and through which they went into the world as agents of the love of God in Christ.

We can follow that pattern across the whole history of the Christian faith. Whenever and wherever the church has been most alive and most effective, it has always followed that twofold pattern of (1) the gathered congregation for worship and (2) small groups for learning, caring, and ministry in the world.

I never would have made it without a small group of men around me who sustained me all the time. I would never be making it today without brothers in Christ.
　　　　—Charles Colson, Christianity Today, *March 12, 1976, p. 5*

This pattern of community was at the heart of the Wesleyan revival in England in the eighteenth century. Historians gained an intensive look into the life of early Methodism when Duke University professor Richard Heitzenrater discovered the journal of Benjamin Ingham. Ingham was a member of one of the small groups at Oxford University led by John and Charles Wesley. The movement grew out of a gnawing hunger for a deeper, more vital relationship with God—an inner desire to fulfill the Great Commandment to love God with all your heart, soul, mind, and strength, and to love your neighbors as you love yourself. To reach that goal, members of "The Holy Club" became more diligent in the traditional spiritual disciplines. They received the sacrament of Holy Communion each day in the university chapels. They gathered regularly in small groups of six or eight to study the Scriptures and the writings of spiritual leaders in church history. They held one another accountable for their spiritual discipline and their common life of prayer. From those small groups they went to the jails, workhouses, and slums of Oxford. They prayed with prisoners, tutored children, offered rudimentary medical care, and preached the gospel to people who were not welcome in the established churches.

Fellow students mocked their disciplined and methodical life by calling them "Methodists." And those of us who have followed in their line have been called that ever since, even when we have failed to live up to their discipline and spiritual vitality.

Void If Detached means that each disciple of Jesus must find her or his place to belong in the company of other members of the Body of Christ. It also means that we are connected with the long line of Christian disciples in the church. From a New Testament perspective, we may be religious without the church, but we can never be genuinely, fully, effectively Christian without a connection to other Christians in the Body of Christ.

But let's tell the truth: the church as we know it seldom lives up to the New Testament standard. While there is widespread interest in Jesus today, there is an equally widespread lack of interest in the institutional church. In the sixteenth century, Martin Luther voiced the feelings of many people today when he said that he would not have such a difficult time with Christ if he did not bring along his "leprous bride," the church. Many of us who are most committed to "the old ship of Zion" are often tempted to feel that being in the church is just like being in Noah's ark—we endure the stench on the inside because of fear of the flood on the outside.

Dr. George Foster was one of the mentor-pastors for my ministry. He joined "the church triumphant" years ago, but I can still see the twinkle in his eye and hear the chuckle in his voice when he recited this ditty:

> To be there above with the people we love—
>   That will be glory.
> To be here below with the people we know—
>   That's another story!

The church isn't perfect, because it is filled with imperfect people like every one of us. I decided a long time ago that a church in which everyone was just like me would be far too small to make any real difference in this world. We are a very human bunch! But the writer of Hebrews said that the rest of the church without us—and we without them—will not be made perfect. We will never fulfill God's vision without one another. This sometimes hulking, sometimes stumbling, sometimes spectacular, always human body that we call the church is the ongoing line through which the kingdom reign and rule of God is modeled in this world. Bill Hybels has shaped the vision of the Willow Creek Community Church and the global influence of the Willow Creek Association of churches around a passionate conviction that "the church is the hope of the world."

Without Jesus there can be no church; and without the church we cannot stay united with Jesus. I've yet to meet anyone who has come closer to Jesus by forsaking the church.
                    —Henri Nouwen, Letters to Marc About Jesus, *p. 83*

Jesus used a vivid agricultural metaphor to describe just how critical this connection is for the spiritual survival of the disciple: "I am the vine, you are the branches. Those who abide in me and I in them bear much fruit, because apart from me you can do nothing. Whoever does not abide in me is thrown away like a branch and withers. . . . If you abide in me, and my words abide in you . . . you [will] bear much fruit" (John 15:5-8).

You know what happens when a branch is cut off from the vine. It may look green for a while, but eventually it will wither and die. It cannot sustain itself without drawing its life from the vine. Like that branch, we are "void if detached." We need to be connected to each other in the life of the church.

The great mystery in all of this is that our connection is not limited to the church here on earth. It extends from the present into the past and into the future. It reaches beyond our human experience of the church on earth into the fulfillment of the church in heaven. It extends through life, beyond death, into life everlasting. By faith we believe that we are connected with those who have gone before us into life eternal.

I hadn't thought much about saints; they seemed a Catholic thing, impossibly holy people. But I was learning to see them as witnesses to our

limitations and God's vast possibilities (as well as sense of humor), as Christian theology torn from the page and brought to life.
—*Kathleen Norris,* The Cloister Walk, *pp. 206-7*

I grew up in a staunchly Protestant, pre–Vatican II world where we Protestants knew very little about what went on in the Roman Catholic church down the street. We knew just enough to know that we didn't believe what they believed, particularly all that business about saints. But times have changed. Years of pastoral experience have given me a deeper appreciation for what is happening when a worshiping congregation stands together to affirm the words of the Apostles' Creed: "I believe in . . . the communion of saints." I can't fully explain it. It's a mystery to me. But year by year, as I have shared in the reality of death and the hope of resurrection with people who have been a part of the connected community of faith on earth, I become more convinced that we continue to participate in that connection with them in heaven.

In the congregation I serve, All Saints' Day has become one of the high moments of worship in the Christian year. On the November Sunday closest to November 1, our traditional worship services begin with the choir entering the sanctuary to the mystical sounds of a soft chant. Bearing lighted candles, they surround the congregation. With the ringing of a bell, we call out the names of those church members who have died in the past year and light a candle for each name. Those candles, joined with those held by the choir, surround the gathered church with the witness of those who have joined the church triumphant. Then we hear the words from the Epistle to the Hebrews: "Therefore, since we are surrounded by so great a cloud of witnesses, let us also lay aside every weight and the sin that clings so closely, and let us run with perseverance the race that is set before us, looking to Jesus the pioneer and perfecter of our faith" (Heb. 12:1-2).

The trumpets blow, the organ begins to roll, and we join in singing "For All the Saints Who from Their Labors Rest." I never fail to feel the presence of those who have gone before us when we sing, "O blest communion, fellowship divine! / We feebly struggle, they in glory shine; / yet all are one in thee, for all are thine" (William Walsham How, 1864).

In ways that go beyond easy explanation, I have come to believe in the communion of saints, to feel something of what the writer of the Hebrew epistle meant when he pointed back across all the generations of faith and said, "Yet all these, though they were commended for their faith, did not receive what was promised, since God had provided something better so that they would not, apart from us, be made perfect" (11:39-40).

We, along with them, are void if detached.

Come, let us join our friends above who have obtained the prize,
and on the eagle wings of love to joys celestial rise.
Let saints on earth unite to sing with those to glory gone,
for all the servants of our King in earth and heaven are one.

One family we dwell in him, one church above, beneath,
though now divided by the stream, the narrow stream of death.
—Charles Wesley, "Come, Let Us Join Our Friends Above"
in The United Methodist Hymnal, *no. 709*

How to Find Your Connection

1. What is your deepest experience of friendship? How would you describe the essential elements of that relationship?

2. When have you felt "detached," alone, or isolated, particularly in regard to your faith? Have you ever sensed a connection to the people of faith who have gone before you? If so, describe that connection.

3. How does the assertion that "individual Christianity is a self-contradiction" fit with your understanding of Christian faith?

4. Have you ever experienced anything like the "house church" of the New Testament or the small groups of the early Methodists? What would excite or frighten you about that kind of gathering? Are you searching for this kind of commitment? Are you ready for it? Why or why not?

5. How have you experienced the "communion of saints" as described in this chapter?

Resources for Making Connections

Cordeiro, Wayne. *Doing Church as a Team*. Ventura, Calif.: Regal, 2001.
Heitzenrater, Richard P. *Wesley and the People Called Methodists*. Nashville: Abingdon Press, 1995.
Hunter, George G. *Church for the Unchurched*. Nashville: Abingdon Press, 1996.
Hybels, Lynn and Bill. *Rediscovering Church*. Grand Rapids: Zondervan, 1997.
Morris, Danny and Charles M. Olsen. *Discerning God's Will Together*. Nashville: Upper Room, 1996.
Norris, Kathleen. *The Cloister Walk*. New York: Riverhead Books, 1996.

CHAPTER TEN

Generously Living:
Getting the Title Clear

We must break with a culture that's gone bananas over money.
It's a deeply religious matter.
  —*William Sloane Coffin, from a sermon preached at Riverside*
                      Church, New York, November 10, 1985

In preparation for writing a book on men's spirituality, I spent the larger part of a year in the company of David, the Old Testament hero who ruled over Israel a millennium before the birth of Christ. As I preached my way through his story, I participated in a small group with eight or ten other men who discussed the biblical texts over coffee and doughnuts. We revisited the familiar boyhood stories of David playing his harp, tending his sheep, and slaying Goliath. We felt the poignant pain in his eloquent elegies following the deaths of his mentor/enemy King Saul, his best friend Jonathan, and his rebellious son Absalom. We heard again the story of David's lusty abuse of power in his affair with Bathsheba and in the murder of her husband, Uriah. We watched the disastrous consequences of David's choices unfold with all the marks of a Shakespearean tragedy. It was very powerful stuff. With David, we found ourselves on a journey to the center of our relationship with God and into the center of our own beings.

When we came to the closing scenes of David's life in 1 Chronicles, I told my congregation that I was tempted to put a warning label on the scripture lesson: "WARNING: The Surgeon General has determined that these texts could be dangerous to your *wealth*." I felt as though the sermon needed one of those prime-time television disclaimers, which are carefully crafted, of course, to ensure the rapt attention of every adolescent kid in the house: "PARENTAL DISCRETION ADVISED: These texts contain material that could be dangerous to the social acceptability of your children."

The great King David's last words (found in 1 Chr. 29:10-22) are nothing less than a frontal assault on the most widely accepted and fiercely held assumptions of our culture. They describe a way of living that is a radical alternative to the lifestyle of the mall-addicted, money-adoring, me-oriented society around us. Although they were recorded centuries before Jesus' birth, David's words define a distinguishing mark of those who live under the rule of the kingdom of God revealed in Jesus. If taken seriously, they demand a fundamental rethinking of the central priorities of our existence. The challenge within them goes to the center of our being with the promise and hope of genuine freedom and great joy.

Compulsive extravagance is a modern mania. The contemporary lust for "more, more, more" is clearly psychotic; it has completely lost touch with reality.
　　　　　　　—*Richard Foster,* The Challenge of the Disciplined Life, *p. 5*

Before looking at David's words, I invite you to participate in a practical object lesson. Reach into your pocket or purse and pull out your wallet. Hold it in your hand. Feel it. Now open it and take an inventory of what is inside.

The first thing I see in my wallet is a picture of my wife and daughters. It reminds me of the most important relationships in my life. Next is a driver's license. It isn't just for driving anymore. It is the basic photo-identification card in America. This time my picture actually isn't too bad! My Social Security card is in there. Long after the government trust fund runs out of money, we'll still need the numbers to let computers know who we are! My business card identifies the career in which I spend my life. My voter registration card means I'm an active part of the democratic process in this country. My health insurance card represents one of the most complex issues in our country today, but it is also a reminder that I am called to take care of my body, to maintain my physical health. And then, of course, I find my credit cards. More than 1.1 billion pieces of plastic from 7,000 different banks or companies pack consumer wallets in America today. The typical user carries an average of six or seven separate cards. Finally, in the back, there is some cold, hard cash. When I know there isn't any cash in my wallet, I feel insecure and vulnerable.

Taken as a whole, my wallet tells you more about who I am than any other single possession I own. Get your hands on it, and you have your hands on the most important stuff in my life. That's why I protect it so carefully. When I'm on a crowded city street or riding in a subway, I check the button on my back pants pocket—in which I keep my wallet—with almost obsessive regularity. When I travel in a foreign country, I tuck my wallet into a security pouch around my waist, along with my passport.

I first experienced the wallet object lesson when John Ortberg led us through it in a pastor's conference. At the end of the wallet inventory, he asked each of us to hand our wallet to the person beside us. Nervous laughter filled the room. I found myself keeping my eye on my wallet the entire time it was out of my hand, and this was in a crowd of preachers! I felt a strange invasion of privacy in taking another person's wallet in my hand. When we were all nervously holding someone else's wallet, he gave us comic relief by saying, "Now that you are holding someone else's wallet, we are going to receive the offering. I encourage you to give the way you've always believed people should give." We laughed, but we were all more comfortable when we each had our own wallet back in our hands!

Jesus never carried a wallet. He didn't even have pockets! But he was talking about what the wallet represents when he said, "Do not store up for yourselves treasures on earth, where moth and rust consume and where thieves break in and steal; but store up for yourselves treasures in heaven, where neither moth nor rust consumes and where thieves do not break in and steal. For where your treasure is, there your heart will be also" (Matt. 6:19-21).

My wallet represents my treasure, the heart and soul of my existence. It contains the tangible expressions of the things I prize the very most. The question the wallet inventory raises goes to the center of our being: Who really owns it? Your life, your career, your time, your relationships, your loyalties, your money—who owns them?

The secular world knows the answer to that question. I own it! It's *mine*, all *mine!* If you question my title to this piece of property, I can go to court to prove it belongs to me. If you threaten my ownership, this society tells me that I even have a right to use a gun to shoot you. Everything around us conditions us to believe that we own it!

It is preoccupation with possession more than anything else that prevents men from living freely and nobly.
—*Bertrand Russell, as quoted in* Whatever Became of Sin? *p. 149*

Former baseball catcher and television sportscaster Joe Garagiola tells the story of a critical moment in a game against St. Louis when Stan Musial came to the plate. Musial was at the peak of his career and could hit almost anything out of the park. The pitcher was nervous. Garagiola called for a fastball, but the pitcher shook his head. Garagiola then signaled a curve. Again the pitcher shook him off. The pitcher resisted everything he called. Finally, Garagiola marched out to the mound and said, "I've called every pitch in the book; what do you want to throw?" The pitcher replied, "Nothing. I just want to hold on to this thing as long as I can."

The world conditions me to hold on to everything my wallet represents as tightly and as long as I can. Hoard it, save it, invest it, protect it, at all costs. The irony is that when I act as though I own all this stuff, the things I own begin to take ownership of me. The more committed I am to the things I own, the more of myself I must invest to protect them, care for them, enhance them, or serve them. Pretty soon, my possessions begin to take possession of me.

I used to think that Christ might have been exaggerating when he warned about the dangers of wealth. Today I know better. . . . Money has a dangerous way of putting scales on our eyes, a dangerous way of freezing people's hands, eyes, lips, and hearts.
—*Archbishop Dom Helder Camara, as quoted by William Sloane Coffin Jr. in* Sermons, *October 20, 1985*

One *Time* magazine cover article on credit-card debt was titled "Strings Attached" (October 14, 1996, p. 70). It described the way lenders are banking on credit cards to make huge profits by encouraging card users to pile up mountains of debt. One company even became the first to announce a $25 annual penalty for consumers who avoid steep interest charges by paying off their balances every month. In credit-industry parlance, those folk are called "deadbeats." And all these years I thought that paying off your debts was what it meant to be a responsible consumer!

Pastoral experience confirms that multitudes of people are discovering that there are "strings attached" to all the easy credit, as the binge of "buy-now, pay-later" debt begins to take control of their lives. I'm generally skeptical about most of what I hear people say about demons. But I have become convinced that there is something profoundly demonic about the way young adults, long before they have a stable income, are lured into the bottomless pit of high-interest debt to satisfy the insatiable greed of corporate bankers. There is demonic power in the way our children are conditioned to believe that they can and should have whatever they want, the instant they want it, without regard to when or how they will pay for it. In this culture, the most common form of demonic possession is the way our possessions take possession of us.

The problem is not that the young people haven't learned our values; it's that they have. They can see beneath our social and religious platitudes to what we care about most.
—*Jim Wallis,* The Soul of Politics, *p. 127*

Who owns it? The Bible offers a radical alternative to the world's answer to that question. We hear it in the way David prayed:

"Blessed are you, O LORD, the God of our ancestor Israel, forever and ever. Yours, O LORD, are the greatness, the power, the glory, the victory, and the majesty; for all that is in the heavens and on the earth is yours; yours is the kingdom, O LORD, and you are exalted as head above all. Riches and honor come from you, and you rule over all. In your hand are power and might; and it is in your hand to make great and to give strength to all. And now, our God, we give thanks to you and praise your glorious name.

"But who am I, and what is my people, that we should be able to make this freewill offering? For all things come from you, and of your own have we given you. For we are aliens and transients before you, as were all our ancestors; our days on the earth are like a shadow, and there is no hope. O LORD our God, all this abundance that we have provided for building you a house for your holy name comes from your hand and is all your own." (1 Chr. 29:10-16)

It would be hard to miss the enormous inclusivity of that little word *all*. It shows up eight times in these seven verses. Biblical faith declares that God owns it *all*.

All that is in the heavens and on the earth is yours.
You are exalted as head above *all*.
You rule over *all*.
You give strength to *all*.
All things come from you.
We are transients before you, as were *all* our ancestors.
All this abundance . . . comes from your hand and is *all* your own.

The Bible says that all the stuff represented in our wallets—and a whole lot more!—belongs to God. People who are on a journey to the center of the faith build their lives on the basic assumption that all that they have is a gift. It is all on loan to them from a generous God. All that they have is to be used in ways that are consistent with the rule, will, and way of God revealed in Jesus Christ.

In every congregation we have served, our family has been blessed by generous folk who have offered us the use of their vacation homes as a place to rest, recuperate, and renew our souls. I allow my memory to ramble back to a beachfront condo on the Atlantic Ocean, a cabin in the Great Smoky Mountains, a house on the Gulf of Mexico. In each house, we felt the presence of its actual owner. The pictures on the walls, the books on the shelves, the furniture in the rooms— all reminded us of the presence of the people who owned the place in which we were privileged to reside for a little while.

In the same way, people of biblical faith look on everything around them as the reminder, the sign and symbol, of the One who holds the ultimate title to everything. The culture around us determines our "worth" on the basis of what we own. But in contrast, David declares that we are "aliens and transients." At best we are short-term tenants, temporary custodians of things that ultimately belong to God. Our value is determined not by what we own but by our relationship with the Owner.

Legends abound about a monument to the memory of Cornelius O'Brien that stands in the town square of the little village of Liscannor, on the west coast of Ireland. One legend says that the nineteenth-century mayor was a rapacious man who acquired most of his wealth by lending to the poor people of the village at outrageous interest and foreclosing when they couldn't pay. Another legend numbers his good deeds for the village. Some say he erected the huge obelisk in his own honor, while others say it was placed there by his admirers. Everyone agrees that he was rich. One of the best-known stories is that during his funeral, the boys of the village gathered in the local pub to lift a pint over his passing. One villager asked, "How much did old O'Brien leave?" The bartender replied, "Begorra, he left all of it!"

And so will every one of us. The Bible is quick to remind us that we are, at best, short-term custodians of things that ultimately belong to God. We hold them in our hands for a while, but then we are gone. Shrouds have no pockets; hearses don't have trailer hitches. At the end, we leave it all behind. In the meanwhile, we are called to use everything we hold in ways that are consistent with the will and purpose of the owner, which means ordering everything in our lives around the kingdom and rule of God.

John Ortberg described this principle in a sermon that has already become something of a classic. He remembered the day he finally beat his grandmother in a game of Monopoly. As he gloated over his empire of railroads and utilities, of streets and avenues loaded with houses and hotels, his grandmother gently reminded him that at the end of the game it all goes back in the box. And at the end, so do we.

A steward is an apt description of every human being from Adam to you and me, for while each of us has been given the responsibility for the management of something absolutely awesome—this wonderful, terrible, beautiful world—yet we must recognize at the same time that it belongs to another.
—William Sloane Coffin, Sermons, *October 23, 1983*

If we believe that God actually owns all of it and that we are to bring all of our resources under the rule and authority of God, the question that confronts us is not *How much of what I own will I give to God?* The question becomes *How much of what God owns will I keep for myself?* The question is not *How much of what I own will I allow to be used for God's purpose?* The question is *How much of what I have in my care will I dare to use for anything less than those things that are in accord with God's will and God's purpose in my life?*

No wonder David prays for his people! He acknowledges God's greatness, God's glory, and God's authority and rule over all, and then he prays, "Keep forever such purposes and thoughts in the hearts of your people, and direct their hearts toward you" (1 Chr. 29:18).

The word we use to describe the practical process of ordering our resources around the rule and will of God is *stewardship*. This is a word that, unfortunately, has been cheapened by its use, so that folk who are familiar with it at all immediately think that it means raising money for the church. Contrary to that perspective, the biblical purpose of Christian stewardship is not to raise money for the church but to get our lives right with God. Jesus put the issue before us just as clearly and contentiously as he could: "No one can serve two masters; for a slave will either hate the one and love the other, or be devoted to the one and despise the other. You cannot serve God and wealth" (Matt. 6:24).

In the place of the word *wealth*, the more traditional translations use the word *mammon*, which comes off as a religious word with very little practical meaning for us. *Mammon* means "wealth" or "money." The contemporary translations put it out there as clearly as possible: "You cannot serve both God and money." We will never be in right relationship with God until we get our heads and our hearts right about God's relationship with our money.

Mammon is a power that seeks to dominate us. . . . Mammon makes a bid for our hearts. Mammon asks for our allegiance in a way that sucks the milk of human kindness out of our very being.
　　—Richard Foster, The Challenge of the Disciplined Life, *p. 26*

Martin Luther, the leader of the Reformation in the sixteenth century, is often credited with saying that every Christian needs three conversions: a conversion of the heart, a conversion of the mind, and a conversion of the purse. The conversion of the purse involves a ruthless rethinking of what we actually need in contrast to what we have been conditioned to want. It grows out of a shared accountability to other growing Christian persons. It expresses itself in a growing sense of compassion and justice for the poor and in an increasing generosity with all of our resources in the spirit of Christ.

A poll by the Gallup organization revealed what some of us already suspected, namely, that there is a steady increase in the number of persons in America who give nothing to charity. In 1995, only 69 percent of the households reported giving anything to charity, compared to 73 percent in 1993 and 75 percent in 1989. The survey found a similar pattern in volunteerism, with only 49 percent reporting volunteer activities (*The Tampa Tribune*, Oct. 10, 1996, p. 4). In a time of shrinking governmental resources for human needs and declining voluntary charity, one of the distinguishing marks of those who live with Jesus at the center of their lives will be their generosity. They are people who choose to freely give themselves to others in the spirit of Christ.

Christians don't give because they have received material blessings. Christians give even when they have not received material blessings. . . . They give generously because they pattern their life after the example of Christ.

—Mark Trotter, *"When Something Is Missing,"* sermon preached February 7, 1982

In 1 Chronicles 29, it should come as no surprise that after preaching that kind of sermon and praying that kind of prayer, David received an offering! All the people shared in a great day of worship and sacrifice. The story ends with this note of celebration: "They ate and drank before the LORD on that day with great joy" (v. 22). Stewardship always results in joy. In fact, the most joyful people I know are those who have learned to give. We will never

discover the full joy and vitality of the life of faith until we settle the issue of ownership and bring all of our resources under the control of the loving rule and gracious authority of God revealed in Jesus Christ.

I preached on this passage of scripture one Sunday. Later that week I received a letter from a teenager in the congregation who really seemed to get the point.

Dear Rev. Harnish:

I am so glad that I was fortunate enough to hear your sermon today. When I was a child I used to get such great joy out of giving. Since I have gotten older that joy has worn off some. I wanted to know why that had happened because I missed that joy. Well, you pointed it out to me today. I had become too attached to my possessions because I was engulfed in the idea that possessions are a measure of a person's success. In thinking that, I forgot what really mattered. Today I learned that in the eyes of God the true measure of my success is how I am on the inside, how I am toward the people around me, and how committed I am toward leading a life of faith. I also learned that God is the ultimate owner and in heaven what I had on earth won't be important, but what will be important is what I gave. In realizing this today, I got the joy of giving back! And I'm so much happier!

The writer of that letter had found the answer to the question, Who owns it?

Have *you?*

How to Decide Who Owns It

1. Go through your wallet or purse. Reflect on the meaning that each item you find has for you.

2. Read Matthew 6:19-21. What do your wallet, your checkbook, and your credit card statements say about where you place your treasure?

3. What practical difference does it make for you to believe that "God owns it"? What does it mean for you to see yourself as a steward of things that ultimately belong to God?

4. How much are you giving away as an act of Christian steward-ship? Are you satisfied with your level of giving? Why or why not?

5. How have you experienced the joy of giving? What is God calling you to give as a witness of your commitment to Christ?

Resources for Creative Stewardship

Capon, Robert Farrar. *Health, Money and Love & Why We Don't Enjoy Them*. Grand Rapids: Eerdmans, 1990.

Foster, Richard J. *Celebration of Discipline*. San Francisco: HarperSanFrancisco, 1988.

———. *The Challenge of the Disciplined Life*. San Francisco: HarperSanFrancisco, 1985.

Frank, Robert H., and Philip J. Cook. *The Winner-Take-All-Society*. New York: Martin Kessler Books, 1995.

Sojourners. *Who Is My Neighbor?* Washington, D.C.: Sojourners, 1996.

Wallis, Jim. *The Soul of Politics*. New York, N.Y. and Maryknoll, N.Y.: The New Press and Orbis Books, 1994.

CHAPTER ELEVEN

Patiently Peaceful:
Planting the Seeds of Peace

Come, behold the works of the LORD;
. . . .
He makes wars cease to the end of the earth;
he breaks the bow, and shatters the spear;
he burns the shields with fire. (Ps. 46:8-9).

"The kingdom of God is as if someone would scatter seed on the
ground . . . and the seed would sprout and grow." (Mark 4:26-27)

Seeds. Just tiny, windblown seeds. But somewhere, some-
time—who knows when?—those seeds fell into a microscopic
crevice in a huge wall of rock jutting out along a trail in the Rocky
Mountain National Park. Over the years, multitudes of hikers have
passed that spot. Most of them never noticed the small, green shoot
that emerged from that tiny crack. But now—God only knows how
many decades later!—it is impossible to miss the majestic pine that
has split the rock and continues to rise toward the sun.

Jesus said that the kingdom of God—the alternative community
of those whose lives are centered in the will and way of God
revealed in Jesus—is like a seed dropped into a crevice in the rock,
along the road, or into the rich soil of life (Matt. 13:1-9). The writer
of the New Testament Letter of James described them as seeds "the
peacemakers plant in peace" (James 3:18 TEV). If we take the
words of Jesus as our travel guide on the way to the center of the
faith, sooner or later we must deal with his claim that peacemakers are the children of God (Matt. 5:9).

If anyone should ask you what are the most radical words in the gospel, you
need not hesitate to reply: "Love your enemies."
                    —Henri Nouwen, Letters to Marc About Jesus, *p. 54*

When it comes to peacemaking, the followers of Jesus are seed planters for a vision they may never live to see fulfilled. Farmers who plant corn see their crop in one season, but people who work for peace are tree farmers who know that they are in for a long haul. People who journey to the center of life in Christ are called to be patient seed planters of peace in an increasingly violent world.

The gospel call to nonviolence and peacemaking is clearly out of synch with the common assumptions of the world in which we live. A preacher-friend in California told me that several years ago, when the legislature was debating a proposition banning capital punishment, Mother Teresa called the governor to suggest that he do what Jesus would do. One of the newspapers heard about the call and published an editorial with the headline "Mother Teresa, Butt Out!" Although we do it much more politely, one of the great ironies of American Christianity is that many people who hold a high view of the inspiration and authority of scripture have been unbelievably adept at finding polite ways to say, "Jesus, butt out!" on Jesus' call to nonviolence. But if we believe that the words recorded in the Gospel narratives are even a close approximation of the actual words of Jesus, what will we do with these?

> "You have heard that it was said, 'You shall love your neighbor and hate your enemy.' But I say to you, Love your enemies and pray for those who persecute you, so that you may be children of your Father in heaven; for he makes his sun rise on the evil and on the good, and sends rain on the righteous and on the unrighteous. For if you love those who love you, what reward do you have? Do not even the tax collectors do the same? And if you greet only your brothers and sisters, what more are you doing than others? Do not even the Gentiles do the same? Be perfect, therefore, as your heavenly Father is perfect." (Matt. 5:43-48)

If we claim the Bible as the central authority for our life and faith, how do we respond to this directive from the apostle Paul?

> Bless those who persecute you; bless and do not curse them. . . . Do not repay anyone evil for evil, but take thought for what is noble in the sight of all. If it is possible, so far as it depends on you, live peaceably with all. Beloved, never avenge yourselves, but leave room for the wrath of God; for it is written, "Vengeance is mine, I will repay, says the Lord." No, "if your enemies are hungry, feed

them; if they are thirsty, give them something to drink; for by doing this you will heap burning coals on their heads." Do not be overcome by evil, but overcome evil with good. (Rom. 12:14-21)

Christians have, on the whole, simply ignored this teaching.
　　　　　　　　　　—*Walter Wink,* Engaging the Powers, *p. 175*

The spiritual tradition in which my faith was formed conditioned me to neutralize Jesus' call to nonviolence by transforming it into a spiritual principle that we were never expected to actualize in real, human experience. Along the way, however, a few isolated disciples planted seeds of Christ-centered nonviolence in my life. Those seeds took root, and they have continued to grow within me across the years.

As I have mentioned before, I was a member of the graduating high-school class of 1965. My rock-ribbed Republican family supported Barry Goldwater for president. The only thing I knew for sure about the war in Vietnam was that those who protested against it were wrong. Because I attended a conservative Christian college, I was largely unaffected by the turmoil on the rest of the campuses in America. Then, during my second year in seminary, a broad-based coalition of anti-war groups called for a nationwide moratorium against the war. The symbol of the moratorium was a black armband.

I still remember the jolt that went through my system when my New Testament Greek professor walked into our class wearing a white armband as a symbol of life, rather than black as a symbol of death. He was the first honest-to-goodness, flesh-and-blood Christian pacifist to cross my path. The fact that, having grown up in the church and having attended a Christian college, I was in seminary before I met a persuasive witness for nonviolence is my personal measure of the general denial of this part of the gospel in American Christianity.

When confronted about his witness for peace, he simply said that his study of the New Testament had convinced him that the way of war was incompatible with the way of Jesus. For him to be a faithful follower of Jesus, he believed he had no choice. It was not an issue of politics for him; it was about faithful obedience to the way of Jesus. He did not arrogantly impose his convictions on us. I was free to agree or disagree, but I could not ignore the integrity of his simple desire to be a faithful follower of Christ. The seed had been planted. My growth toward Christian nonviolence began.

Christians are peacemakers, not because they cannot fight, but because they prefer the force of peace.
                    —*Oscar Romero, quoted in* Peace Prayers, *p. 30*

❖

Two decades later, my journey intersected with the Methodist Order of Peacemakers in South Africa. I watched them model Jesus' way of peacemaking in a cauldron of violence. I prayed with them as they supported young men who faced prosecution as conscientious objectors. I heard the stories of police beatings and imprisonment because some dared to question the violent authority of the apartheid regime. With fearful hesitation, I stood with them on a Johannesburg picket line as they called for an end to military conscription. Their peaceful strength, warm acceptance, and courageous faith forced me to struggle with what it might mean to actually live under the authority of Jesus' words in the Sermon on the Mount. They introduced me to the Gospel commentaries of Walter Wink that helped me hear the Sermon on the Mount in a refreshingly practical way.

When I returned from South Africa, I offered an invitation for people who wanted to study Jesus' way of peacemaking to gather with me. Those who responded were a fascinating and diverse group. They included a retired businessman, two retired schoolteachers, a 1960s civil-rights activist whose commitment to nonviolence had been dormant for two decades, a teenager who simply wanted to follow Jesus, and a physician who was searching for a deeper faith.

We knew that none of us had all of the answers to the complex economic and political issues that converge in what Dwight Eisenhower so prophetically called "the military-industrial complex." But we shared a common hunger for peace. We told our stories, studied the Scriptures, and read the words of Gandhi, Martin Luther King Jr., Dorothy Day, Thomas Merton, and Daniel Berrigan. We prayed together. We experienced the presence of Jesus in our fellowship in a profound way. In the amazing providence of God, we were prepared to be witnesses for God's vision of peace in the stressful days surrounding the war in the Persian Gulf.

About this time, I spent a year of study in the Minor Prophets of the Old Testament. Their vision of *shalom*, their passion for justice, and their profound confidence in the goodness of God enlarged my understanding of the kingdom of God in ways that reinforced my growing commitment to nonviolence as a central part of the divine purpose that Jesus modeled for us. The seeds continued to grow, and their roots began to spread.

I am a solider of Christ; I cannot fight.
—*St. Martin of Tours, quoted in* Peace Prayers, *p. 122*

Mahatma Gandhi used the phrase "soul force." Martin Luther King Jr. showed us the way of "nonviolent resistance." Harry Emerson Fosdick preferred the Quaker term "Christian pacifism." E. Stanley Jones proclaimed the gospel of "unquenchable good will, the law of love in human relationships." Under different labels, they bore witness to the radical alternative of the Christian gospel in a violent world. As the seeds of peacemaking have grown within my own experience, I have been led to several principles that continue to nurture those roots in my life.

1. *Christian peacemaking is always Christ-centered.* It is defined by the "foolishness" and "weakness" of the cross (see 1 Cor. 1:18-31).

Christian nonviolence is born out of a simple and passionate desire to be like Jesus: to live on the basis of his love, to be faithful to his command, to act in ways that are consistent with his vision of the kingdom, and to experience the love with which he went to the cross. At the cross we see the deadly power of violence, and in the Resurrection we know the triumphant power of suffering love.

Were it not for the cross, the world's addiction to violent power would make sense to me. It is, in fact, an almost reasonable alternative in a broken, sinful, and God-forsaking world. But in the self-giving love of the cross, God demonstrated a totally different way of dealing with evil. It is the way of redemptive suffering. The way of nonviolence that Jesus chose when he went to the cross is the way of self-giving love that both undermines the assumptions of power in our world and defines the way God chooses to be with us. Jesus calls his disciples to take up that same cross and follow him.

The cross marks the failure, not of God, but of violence.
— *Walter Wink*, Engaging the Powers, *p. 140*

Christian peacemaking begins in our own souls, in the deep places of our human psyche where we wrestle with anger, hostility, and violent emotions. It is the outward expression of an inner life of peace that is nurtured by a growing relationship with Christ. It simply will not do to attempt to bear witness to peacemaking with an angry spirit. Like everything else in a Christian person's life, such witness must flow from a center of redemptive love.

2. *Christian peacemaking is active, not passive.*
Unfortunately, the English word *pacifism* sounds a lot like the word *passive*. Nothing could be farther from the truth of the gospel. Jesus never called his disciples to be "passive" in the face of injustice, abuse, or undeserved suffering. Rather, he modeled the way of active, difficult, costly, aggressive goodwill. He calls us to liberate the oppressed, to set captives free, to bring justice and wholeness to lives and relationships, to heal the brokenness in the world that is the hellish pit out of which violence flows.

In the Sermon on the Mount, Jesus commands proactive nonviolence in the face of evil. In his letter to the Roman Christians, Paul challenges us not to be overcome by evil, but to overcome evil with good. The New Testament model is not passivity, but peace-filled action. The way of Christian nonviolence searches for ways of resisting violence without resorting to violence. It is the soul-force that seeks radical change for human relationships. John Dear calls nonviolent resistance "liberating action on behalf of suffering humankind" (*Our God Is Nonviolent*, p. 7).

3. *The goal of Christian peacemaking is not just peace, but a just peace.*
Pope Paul VI said, "If you want peace, work for justice" (quoted in *Peace Prayers*, p. 11). The Old Testament prophets lifted up the vision of *shalom*: the whole created order functioning in harmony with God's purpose. The New Testament uses the word *reconciliation* (2 Cor. 5:19). Martin Luther King Jr. always reminded his followers that the goal of nonviolence is not simply stopping an oppressor, but transforming the oppressor into a friend. He learned that lesson from Gandhi, who said that the ultimate test of nonviolence is that there is no rancor left behind and that in the end, former enemies have been reconciled. Peacemaking always involves preventing violence by searching for justice.

The end is redemption and reconciliation. The aftermath of nonviolence is the creation of the beloved community.
—Martin Luther King Jr., A Testament of Hope, p. 8

4. *Christian peacemakers are as concerned about means as they are about ends.*
The Epistle of James reminds us that we cannot reap olives from a fig tree. What we plant is what we get. Plant violence, we get more violence. Plant seeds of peace, and in time we will reap peace. Christ-followers are convinced that the means they use must be consistent with the ends they seek.
In the aftermath of the 1995 bombing of the Alfred P. Murrah Federal Building in Oklahoma City, I felt called to remind my congregation that Easter people, people who live in the power of the Resurrection, are called by the risen Christ to the way of nonviolence and peace. In the sermon that Sunday, I said, "The perpetrators of this crime must be brought to the bar of justice. But if their act of violence fosters a spirit of vengeance within us, then Satan

will have won. If their act of meanness makes us more mean, then the powers of hell will have triumphed. The only thing more difficult than overcoming evil with good is trying to overcome evil with more evil. When we try to overcome evil with evil, we compound the total amount of evil in the world. The only thing more impossible than overcoming violence with nonviolence is trying to overcome violence with more violence."

The Christ-shaped alternative to the hopeless attempt to overcome evil with evil is a hope-filled passion to overcome evil with good.

❖

Ultimately you can't reach good ends through evil means, because the means represent the seed and the end represents the tree.
 —*Martin Luther King Jr.*, A Testament of Hope, *p. 255*

❖

5. The final—and perhaps most important—principle is that *ultimately, God's goodness and wholeness will prevail over the violence and brokenness of our world.*

Peacemakers are not in a hurry. They dare to believe that they are called to be faithful to the way of Jesus, not because it is immediately successful, but because it is the way in which God will ultimately heal and redeem this creation.

My experience with the Methodist Order of Peacemakers in South Africa continues to nourish the seeds of hope and faith within my soul. Peter J. Storey was one of the founders of that order. As a pastor, as the bishop of the Central District of the Methodist Church in Johannesburg, as the president of the South African Council of Churches, and as a follower of Jesus Christ, he became one of the courageous leaders of the movement that finally brought freedom to South Africa.

I remember hearing Peter tell about a time during some of the most difficult years of the struggle when he realized that it had been thirty years since he stood in his first protest against apartheid. He said that back then he had no idea that one day his sons would still be standing in the same line, still waiting for the day of freedom, justice, and peace. When I asked what kept him going over all those years, he said it was his confidence in the king-dom of God: the deep, inner assurance that God would be faithful and that one day the vision would be fulfilled. He introduced me to a hymn that captures that confident hope in the vision of peace.

> There's a light upon the mountains, and the day is at the spring,
> When our eyes shall see the beauty and the glory of the King;
> Weary was our heart with waiting, and the night-watch seemed so long;
> But His triumph-day is breaking, and we hail it with a song.
>
> There's a hush of expectation, and a quiet in the air;
> And the breath of God is moving in the fervent breath of prayer.
> For the suffering, dying Jesus is the Christ upon the throne,
> And the travail of our spirit is the travail of His own.
>
> He is breaking down the barriers, He is casting up the way;
> He is calling for His angels to build up the gates of day.
> But His angels here are human, not the shining hosts above;
> For the drum-beats of His army are the heart-beats of our love.
>
> Hark! we hear a distant music, and it comes with fuller swell;
> 'Tis the triumph-song of Jesus, of our King, Immanuel.
> Zion, go thou forth to meet Him; and my soul, be swift to bring
> All thy sweetest and thy dearest for the triumph of our King!
> —Henry Burton, from *The School Hymn-Book of the Methodist Church*
> (London: Methodist Youth Department, 1950), p. 491

Seeds. Just seeds. But seeds that peacemakers plant in peace. And if we are patient, we will see the promise within them fulfilled.

I earnestly pray and hope that you will cling to those small signs of hope and not let yourself be led astray by the noise and clamor of those who persist in relying on violence. . . . Let us hope and pray with all our hearts that we may have the courage and the confidence to follow the way of Jesus to the end.

—Henri Nouwen, Letters to Marc About Jesus, *p. 64*

How to Plant Seeds of Peace

1. Read Matthew 5:43-48. What is your honest response to these words from Jesus? Do these words anger, surprise, or inspire you? Explain.

2. Have you had personal contact with people who identified themselves as Christian pacifists? If so, what impact did they have on your life? What are your impressions of the Christian pacifists mentioned in this chapter?

3. Study the principles of peacemaking that are affirmed here. Where can you find yourself in them? Where do they contradict the way you live?

4. Consider being a part of a small group for study and reflection on the theme of Christian nonviolence and peacemaking. What barriers exist for you in making such a commitment? What commitment to the ways of nonviolence and peace are you prepared to make at this time?

5. Where is the place of anger, conflict, or hostility in your own soul that needs to be touched with the peace of Christ? Describe that place. How can you invite Christ inside?

Resources for Christ-Centered Peacemaking

Dear, John. *Our God Is Nonviolent*. New York: The Pilgrim Press, 1990.

Jones, E. Stanley. *Gandhi: Portrayal of a Friend*. Nashville: Abingdon Press, 1993.

Leadingham, Carrie, Joann E. Moschella, and Hilary M. Vartanian, eds. *Peace Prayers: Meditations, Affirmations, Invocations, Poems, and Prayers for Peace*. San Francisco: HarperSanFrancisco, 1992.

Merton, Thomas. *The Nonviolent Alternative*. New York: Farrar, Straus & Giroux, 1980.

Wallis, Jim. *Agenda for Biblical People*. San Francisco: Harper & Row, 1984.

Washington, James Melvin, ed. *A Testament of Hope: The Essential Writings and Speeches of Martin Luther King, Jr.* San Francisco: HarperSanFrancisco, 1986.

Wink, Walter. *Violence and Nonviolence in South Africa*. Philadelphia: New Society Publishers, 1987.

———. *Engaging the Powers: Discernment and Resistance in a World of Domination*. Minneapolis: Fortress Press, 1992.

CHAPTER TWELVE

Deliriously Hopeful: Rejoicing in God's Reign!

The tragedy of life is not death, but what dies inside while we are living. . . . We must recognize that we get our basic energy not from turbines but from hope.
—*Norman Cousins,* Context, *July 15, 1991, p. 3*

He that lives in hope dances without music.
—*George Herbert, quoted in* Dictionary of Quotations *(New York: Delacorte Press, 1968), p. 324*

I couldn't help myself; I had to ask the question. I had listened to the stories people told in the crowded flats of Johannesburg, in the squatter settlements outside of Cape Town, and in a Methodist pastor's humble home in Soweto. I had sensed a tiny measure of the fear and suffering these brothers and sisters in Christ had faced in the struggle for freedom in South Africa. I saw how these very ordinary people had confronted the entrenched evil of apartheid in an absolutely extraordinary way. They had every reason to feel discouraged and defeated. But to be with them was to experience inescapable, contagious joy! Finally, I asked the question: "What keeps you going? How can you be so joyful?" With amazing consistency, they responded with one word: *hope.*

Trevor Huddleston, the Anglican priest who was expelled from South Africa as one of the earliest witnesses for freedom, gave voice to that hope when he wrote: "Optimism . . . is 'not enough.' But *hope* is enough, because it is . . . based on the truth (as we accept it) that this is God's world and not ours" (*Return to South Africa*, p. 138).

Witnesses to the sustaining power of Christian hope are not limited to South Africa. Lance Morrow, writing for *Time* magazine, asked Vaclav Havel what kept him going. The one-time poet of protest and president of the Czech Republic replied:

I cherish a certain hope in me, hope as a state of spirit—a state of spirit without which I cannot imagine living. . . . Hope forces me to believe that those better alternatives will prevail, and above all it forces me to do something to make them happen. (*Time*, August 3, 1992, p. 48)

Moorhead Kennedy, reflecting on the 444 days he was held as a hostage in Iran, said, "In the end, we hostages learned to live on hope" (*The Ayatollah in the Cathedral*, p. 163). As a pastor, I have seen that same kind of hope in the lives of ordinary people who have faced hardship and pain with extraordinary strength. The sustaining power for men and women who are on a journey to the center of the faith is hope—hope that is not dependent on the conditions of the world around them, but hope that is energized by the power of the Resurrection. The apostle Paul declared it in the Letter to the Ephesians:

I pray that the God of our Lord Jesus Christ, the Father of glory, may give you a spirit of wisdom and revelation as you come to know him, so that, with the eyes of your heart enlightened, you may know what is the hope to which he has called you . . . and what is the immeasurable greatness of his power for us who believe, according to the working of his great power. God put this power to work in Christ when he raised him from the dead. (Eph. 1:17-20)

People who hope are people who act in the conviction that God's future is reliably present-tense and therefore act upon it before it is fully in hand. . . . Christians count on the winner who has yet to do the winning.
—Walter Brueggemann, "The Other Side," March/April 1999, quoted in Context, *June 15, 1999, pp. 6-7*

From the balcony of my hotel room in Rio de Janeiro, I could look in one direction and see the spectacular beaches that stretch from Ipanema to Copacabana. Waves crashed in on the rocks. The mosaic-tiled sidewalks were crowded with beautiful people. Sometimes trendy and sometimes tacky hotels lined one of the most beautiful beaches in the world. But when I turned in the opposite direction, I looked up into the largest *favela*—a shantytown or slum—in Brazil. Estimates are that as many as 250,000 people are crowded into the tiny concrete-block huts that are stacked on top of one another on the mountainside like a beehive ("beehive" is the literal translation of the word *favela*). In the middle of the *favela*, the Methodists of Brazil have established an amazing ministry called "The Hope Factory."

High above the city, the magnificent statue of Christ the Redeemer spreads its arms on the top of Corcovado. The figure faces the ocean, which means that its back is toward the *favela*. On one particularly difficult day, a worker in The Hope Factory said that she looked up, saw the back of the statue, and felt for all the world as if Christ had turned his back on the people of the *favela*. Then one of the people reminded her, "He has not turned his back on us; he is leading us out."

The Hope Factory is a tangible expression of what it means to be the community of hope in a broken, pain-racked, and sometimes hostile world. Christian people are called to be the purveyors of hope—hope that is not dependent on the fickle optimism of the world around us, but is centered in the good news of the risen Christ who leads his people toward a new future.

When . . . hope becomes credible, extremists lose their credibility.
—Moorhead Kennedy, The Ayatollah in the Cathedral, *p. 209*

In his theological *tour de force* on the Resurrection in 1 Corinthians 15, Paul opens his argument with the singular historical event of the resurrection of Jesus. As he progresses, his vision expands exponentially. He extends the power of the Resurrection to the lives of all those who belong to Christ. Then Paul soars to the outer limits of human comprehension by describing the impact of the Resurrection upon the whole creation. Finally, he reaches this grand finale: "Then comes the end, when he hands over the kingdom to God the Father, after he has destroyed every ruler and every authority and power. For he must reign until he has put all his enemies under his feet. The last enemy to be destroyed is death. . . . When all things are subjected to him . . . God may be all in all" (1 Cor. 15:24-28).

People on a journey to the center of the faith dare to affirm that the same Jesus who was crucified on Good Friday and raised from the dead on Easter morning is leading us to the future. They rejoice in the hope that one day he will be lifted up as "King of kings and Lord of lords" over the whole creation. They actually believe that the kingdoms of this earth will, in fact, become the kingdom of our God and of his Christ, and he shall reign forever and ever. Now that's a spectacular, cosmic cause for hope! Let's take a look at several elements of that kind of hope.

1. *The Resurrection declares the hope of God's victory over the powers of death.* I watch for some specific people to come to worship on Easter Sunday morning. They enter the building cautiously, just the way the women came to Joseph's tomb, where Jesus' body lay. Their hearts have been broken. Their senses are numb. Their spirits have been anesthetized by the loss of someone they loved more than life itself. For them, there can be no denial of the awesome reality of death. I watch as they sing "Christ the Lord Is Risen Today" with tears in their eyes. For many of them, Charles Wesley's words become their bold declaration of faith in the Resurrection in the face of death.

> Soar we now where Christ has led, Alleluia!
> Following our exalted Head, Alleluia!
> Made like him, like him we rise, Alleluia!
> Ours the cross, the grave, the skies, Alleluia!

Christian people never deny the power of death. Jesus really died on that cross on Friday afternoon. He didn't "pass on" or "go to sleep." He did not, in the words of one satirist, "fail to live up to his wellness expectations." The Apostles' Creed never flinches before the fact that Jesus "was crucified, died, and was buried." But in the place of death, people whose lives are centered in the risen Christ experience the infinitely greater power of life.

Zona was one of God's unique creations. When I was appointed as a brand-new associate pastor to Trinity Church in DeLand, Florida, fresh out of seminary and green as grass, Zona had already been the church secretary for what seemed like about a hundred and fifty years. I soon learned that although I had the degree, she had the experience. She retired while I was there and became our number-one baby-sitter. My daughters are adults now, but they'll always be Zona's babies!

Zona had a sister named Euretta. They grew up at the Florida United Methodist Children's Home when it was an orphanage. Their lives were rooted and centered in the church. Three generations of children had learned Bible stories in Euretta's preschool Sunday school class. While I was her pastor, she turned in her sandbox and retired from teaching. Not long after that, her health began to fail. I remember the morning that Zona called to tell me that it wouldn't be long until Euretta was gone. She ended the conversation by saying, "We're just waiting for her resurrection day, now. She's got her Easter comin'."

Zona's own death came after years of frustration and suffering in the wake of a debilitating stroke. When we gathered in the church that was her home to celebrate her life, I remembered her words about her sister and declared to the congregation, "She's got her Easter comin'!"

Wherever we are on the journey from birth to death to life beyond death, the good news for every one of us is that we have our Easter coming. The Resurrection fills us with hope that the power of God will ultimately be victorious over all the powers of death.

I have often said that when the people stand around and say, "Well, Brother Stanley is gone," I want to be able to wink at them, and if I have enough strength, I would like to laugh and say, "Jesus is Lord." Because this will not be death. It will be fuller life. . . . Because any person who is in Jesus is deathless, for he is under the principle and power of resurrection.

—E. Stanley Jones's *final journal entry before his death,*
in The Divine Yes, *p. 150*

2. *The Resurrection declares the hope of the fulfillment of God's redemptive purpose in creation.* Paul stretches our souls to experience the cosmic vision of the rule of Christ fulfilled throughout the whole of creation (1 Cor. 15:24-28). Because of the Resurrection, we dare to hope that the Way revealed in Jesus—the Way of self-

giving, self-sacrificing love; the Way of truth and compassion; the Way of wholeness and peace; the Way of life described in the Sermon on the Mount; the Way rejected by the rulers and powers of the world and nailed to a cross—will ultimately be vindicated in human history. The Way we see in Jesus will ultimately be fulfilled in every inch of the created order. Take hold of that kind of vision—or let that vision take hold of you!—and this old world will never look the same again.

There is no fragment or particle of the world, which, in the grip of the knowledge of its present misery, does not hope for resurrection.
—*John Calvin, as quoted in Karl Barth's* The Epistle to the Romans, *trans. Edwyn C. Hoskyns (New York: Oxford University Press, 1968), p. 308*

❖

The turning of the millennium created a marketing bonanza for television evangelists and prophecy writers to make a healthy retirement income on the sale of books and videotapes that use the New Testament book of Revelation to predict the end of the world. One book, for instance, was advertised as "a book on Bible prophecy that automatically updates itself every single month!" It offered readers "front-row seats to those very events that will culminate in the soon return of our Lord and Saviour Jesus Christ!" Conservative theologian Richard John Neuhaus pointed out that we must have some time left, because publishers offered reduced rates for three-year magazine subscriptions. He suggested that we need not become too concerned until they start taking subscriptions one month at a time (*Homiletics*, October-December, 1991, p. 30).

The historical fact that every "Bible prophecy" preacher who has set a date for the final coming of Christ has been wrong never seems to deflate the market for their wares. Nor does the direct command of Jesus that we should not be trying to set dates for his return, anyway (Matt. 24:36; Mark 13:32; Acts 1:7). The New Testament images of the final coming of Christ are not given to us to provide a timetable for future events. Their purpose is to wake up somnambulistic saints and to get faithful disciples of Jesus

Christ moving in the right direction. Jesus' parables of the final coming always end with a call for obedient action. The apocalyptic visions of the New Testament call us to start living today the way we'd like to be living when Christ comes again. They challenge us to shape our lives in the present in ways that are consistent with what we believe about the time to come. Because we know the risen Christ will ultimately rule over the whole creation, we are called to model life under his reign right now.

God will bring history to a worthy conclusion when the creation which de jure belongs to God's kingdom will de facto "become the kingdom of our Lord and of his Christ, and he shall reign for ever and ever."
—M. Eugene Boring, Revelation, *p. 2*

3. The Resurrection declares the hope of Christ's risen presence in our present experience. German theologian Jürgen Moltmann wrote that believing in the Resurrection involves more than the affirmation of a fact or mental assent to a doctrine. It means "being possessed by the life-giving Spirit and participating in the powers of the age to come" (*The Way of Jesus Christ*, p. 218). Belief in the Resurrection is not merely affirming that one Sunday morning, nineteen-hundred-odd years ago, God raised Jesus from Joseph's tomb. It means being possessed by the Spirit of the risen Christ today. It is not just affirming the church's doctrine or dogma about the future; it is living as persons through whom the risen life of Jesus is made flesh in the present. It means being part of the Body of Christ through which the infinite, death-denying, life-affirming love of God in Christ is being made real in this world.

While he was the pastor at the Riverside Church in New York, William Sloane Coffin preached an Easter sermon in which he confessed that it is all too easy for us to live as if this were a "Good Friday world." Pick up the paper, watch the evening news, listen to the pain and torment in lives around you—be honest about the sin, the fear, the anxiety in your own soul, and any of us can come to that conclusion. It's easy to believe that this is a world where powerless love is always the victim of loveless power; where only the strong survive and it's every man or woman for him- or herself; where compassion, justice, and peace must be protected by force and destruction; and where joy and laughter are buried in dark tombs of depression, sorrow, or fear. Now and then, all of us are tempted to believe that it's really a Good Friday world after all.

For the past five years I have walked with a faithful Christian brother as he has wrestled his way through a complex and costly struggle. With amazing grace, he has consistently searched for justice, for fairness, and for what would be best for all the persons involved. And with brutal consistency that has a demonic quality about it, things have continued to work against him.

We have often asked ourselves how we ought to pray, and we have always returned to "thy kingdom come, thy will be done on earth as it is in heaven." Along the way we have realized that the Bible never promises that we will necessarily see justice fulfilled in the immediate context of this broken and mean-spirited world. Sometimes we have been tempted to believe that it is really a "Good Friday world," after all.

But in his Easter sermon, William Sloane Coffin went on to declare:

> By the light of Easter . . . we can dimly discern a "Yes, but" kind of message. Yes, fear and self-righteousness, indifference and sentimentality kill; but love never dies, not with God, and not even with us. . . . Christ's resurrection promises our own resurrection, for Christ is risen *pro nobis*, for us, to put love in our hearts, decent thoughts in our heads, and a little more iron up our spines. Christ is risen to convert us, not from life to something more than life, but from something less than life to the possibility of full life itself. (*Living the Truth in a World of Illusions*, p. 70)

Coffin concluded by asking his congregation this reality-defining question: "Are we going to continue the illusion of a Good Friday world, or start living the reality of an Easter one?" (p. 74).

There are a lot of good folk—honest, well-intentioned, many of them people of faith—who live as though this were still a Good Friday world. Their faces give them away; they always look as though they were born in pickle season and raised on vinegar. They go around raining down destruction on every joyful parade. They are bitter folk who always need to have someone or something to fear or hate. They seem to get up every morning asking,

"Who will move this stone?" as though Jesus were still buried in the tomb.

But Easter means that any moment can be the surprise-filled moment of resurrection in which we discover that the stone has already been rolled away! Christ has already been raised! God's victory over evil and suffering and death has already been declared! Amid the painful realities of this "Good Friday world," we can live as those who know the hope of Easter morning. To live by hope is to start living now in ways that are consistent with the new life of the Resurrection. To affirm that "he must reign until he has put all his enemies under his feet" is to know that every day is a new day of resurrection; every moment of our lives is a resurrection moment that can be possessed by the Spirit of the risen Christ.

New creation is beginning in Christ in the very midst of this world of violence and death.
　　　　　　　　　　—*Jürgen Moltmann,* The Way of Jesus Christ, *p. 221*

4. *The result is that the Resurrection enables us to face the future with hope.* The first disciples faced all the painful realities of life head-on. Just read Luke's account of the early church in the book of Acts. They faced persecution, misunderstanding, rejection, suffering, and death. But because of their experience with the risen Christ, they did not hide away in the upper room, moaning about what the world had come to; they went out rejoicing in what had come to the world! They were not depressed by evil, but were energized by hope! They were not afraid of death, but became agents of new life!

In these times, at the dawn of this new millennium, I hear multitudes of people from many different perspectives asking, "What's the world coming to?" In 1954, the Second Assembly of the World Council of Churches declared that the answer to that question had been given to us in the gospel.

To those who ask, "What is coming to the world?" we answer "His Kingdom is coming." To those who ask, "What is in front of us?" we answer, "It is He, the King, who confronts us." To those who ask,

"What may we look forward to?" we answer that we face not a trackless waste of unfilled time with an end that none can dare to predict; we face our living Lord, our Judge and Savior, He who was dead and is alive forevermore, He who has come and is coming and will reign for ever and ever. It may be that we face tribulation; indeed we must certainly face it if we would be partakers with Him. But we know His word, His kingly word: "Be comforted, I have overcome the world." (*Homiletics*, October-December, 1991, p. 29)

Emily Dickinson compared hope to a bird when she wrote: "Hope is the thing with feathers / That perches in the soul" (*Modern American Poetry*, p. 105). The first time I read her words, I thought that comparing hope to a "thing with feathers" meant that it was a flimsy, flighty thing. But then I watched seagulls hold their place in the wind as a tropical storm prepared to blow onto the Florida coast from the Gulf of Mexico. I was amazed at their strength and stability as the sky darkened and the clouds closed in. In fact, they seemed to be enjoying the way the stormy wind lifted their wings as they flew directly into it.

Since then, I have watched people of faith face hard and difficult days. I have seen them weather storms of grief, defeat, discouragement, conflict, and pain. I know that Dickinson got it right. "Hope" is that kind of thing with feathers that soars, unstoppable in the storm. Hope is a song so deep within the soul that nothing can drown out its music. Hope enables us to fly head-on into the wind and allow it to become the force that lifts us to new life.

People who live in the power of the Resurrection begin to discover what Paul meant when he called the resurrection of Jesus "the first fruits" (1 Cor. 15:20). It was just the beginning of God's resurrecting power that will ultimately raise the whole creation to new life. We dare to hope that "as all die in Adam, so all will be made alive in Christ" (v. 22). We dare to hope that "just as we have borne the image of the man of dust, we will also bear the image of the man of heaven" (v. 49). We dare to hope that "when all things are subjected to him . . . God may be all in all" (v. 28). To live by faith is to know the reality of the presence of the risen Christ at work in us as the ultimate reality, the fulfillment of the kingdom that has already been revealed in Jesus Christ.

Nothing that is worth doing can be achieved in our lifetime; therefore we must be saved by hope. Nothing which is true or beautiful or good makes complete sense in any immediate context of history; therefore we must be saved by faith. Nothing we do, however virtuous, can be accomplished alone; therefore we are saved by love.
    —*Reinhold Niebuhr, quoted in* Context, *February 15, 1992, p. 3*

After Christmas each year I hear people say, "Well, it's time to get back to reality." They say it with resignation, as if all the promises of joy, hope, love, and peace that are at the center of the Christmas gospel are little more than a wishful fantasy, a pleasant dream, like sugarplums dancing in our heads. They assume—albeit reluctantly—that the real world is the world about which we read in the newspaper every day: the world of hurt, pain, violence, greed, and war. But people of biblical faith know that reality is exactly the other way around. The ultimate reality, the reality toward which all of history is moving, the lasting reality that God will fulfill at the end of time, is nothing other than God's peaceful kingdom, God's loving reign, God's gracious rule revealed in Jesus Christ. Christian hope is not a wishful fantasy or a pleasant dream. It is a complete awakening to the "real" world in which Jesus Christ reigns and God is all in all! The witness of those who have made the journey to the center of the faith is that it is a joy-soaked way to live, and it is a hope-saturated way to die!

I just carry hope in my heart. . . . Life without hope is an empty, boring, and useless life. I cannot imagine that I could strive for something if I did not carry hope in me. I am thankful to God for this gift. It is as big a gift as life itself.
    —*Vaclav Havel, quoted in* Context, *Feb. 15, 1992, p. 1*

How to Live Hopefully

1. Have you ever known people who caused you to wonder or ask of them, "What keeps you going?" How did those persons answer, or how do you imagine they might answer? What gave them the strength to go on?

2. How have you experienced the power of death? How does the Resurrection provide hope for you in the face of death?

3. Think of a time when you have felt that this is a "Good Friday" world after all. What do you do when you feel that way? How does the Resurrection transform your outlook?

4. What difference would it make in your life for you to be possessed by the life-giving Spirit of the risen Christ and to know that you were participating in the power of the age to come?

5. Where have you experienced the power of hope? How does the promise of the Resurrection empower you to face life right now?

Resources for Hopeful Living

Boring, M. Eugene. *Revelation—Interpretation: A Bible Commentary for Teaching and Preaching*. Louisville.: John Knox Press, 1989.

Coffin, William Sloane. *Living the Truth in a World of Illusions*. San Francisco: Harper & Row, 1985.

Huddleston, Trevor. *Return to South Africa: The Ecstasy and the Agony*. Grand Rapids: Eerdmans, 1991.

Jones, E. Stanley. *The Divine Yes*. Nashville: Abingdon Press, 1975.

Kennedy, Moorhead. *The Ayatollah in the Cathedral*. New York: Hill & Wang, 1986.

Witherington, Ben. *The Realm of the Reign*. Nashville: Discipleship Resources, 1999.